GOATSONG

Phoebe Giannisi was born in Athens. She is the author of eight collections of poetry, including most recently, *Thetis and Aedon* (Kastaniotis, 2021). Her work focuses on the borders between poetry and performance, and investigates the connections of poetics with body and place. She is a Professor of Architecture and Cultural Studies at the University of Thessaly, where she teaches creative writing and curates public poetry performances.

Brian Sneeden is the author of *Last City* (Carnegie Mellon University Press, 2018). His poetry and translations have received the Iowa Review Award in Poetry, an NEA Literature Translation Fellowship, the World Literature Today Translation Prize for Poetry, the Constantinides Memorial Translation Prize and a PEN/Heim Translation Grant. He is a senior lecturer in creative writing and publishing at Manchester Metropolitan University.

'In *Goatsong*, Brian Sneeden's clever, musical translation
introduces English readers to an important new poetic voice.
The first two sections, *Homerica* and *Cicada*, are dreamy
and elemental. Lines swill like waves, occasionally carrying
something sharper onto the shore: a witticism, trash, teeth.
Then comes *Chimera*, a remarkable polyphonic hymn to goats
and the goatself, in which Phoebe Giannsi takes the pastoral
and creates something wild, visceral and wholly new.'
— Clare Pollard, author of *Delphi*

'I was immersed in Phoebe Giannisi's *Goatsong*. I grieved with
her as a mother, and rejoiced with her as a lover of all wild and
wonderful places. Her work lives in me and inspires me to
work harder to capture the truth – as the best poetry always
does.'
— Sasha Dugdale, author of *The Strong Box*

'*Goatsong* intoxicates with its animality of language, gorgeous
lyric and off-kilter metamorphoses, by turns wry, ecstatic and
strange. Reading Phoebe Giannisi is like reading Pre-Socratic
philosophy on all fours, where flies buzz on and off the page
and the polyphony of species and elements is both dazzling
subject and all-encompassing medium.'
— Daisy Lafarge, author of *Paul*

Praise for *Chimera*

'A book that is also an ecosystem, full of impossible crossings
and alive with unexpected communions.'
— Fani Avramopoulou, *antiphony*

'Giannisi is unquestionably herself within a vanguard of
Greek poets for whom self-awareness and honesty have
become second nature.'
— Shon Arieh-Lerer, *World Literature Today*

Fitzcarraldo Editions
133 Rye Lane
London, SE15 4ST
United Kingdom

Copyright © Phoebe Giannisi, 2025
Homerica first published in the USA by World Poetry in 2017
Cicada first published in the USA by New Directions in 2022
Chimera first published in the USA by New Directions in 2024
Translation copyright © Brian Sneeden, 2017, 2022, 2024
This edition first published in the United Kingdom
by Fitzcarraldo Editions in 2025

The right of Phoebe Giannisi to be identified as the author
of this work has been asserted in accordance with
Section 77 of the Copyright, Designs and Patents Act 1988.

ISBN 978-1-80427-189-6

Design by Ray O'Meara
Typeset in Fitzcarraldo
Printed and bound by Pureprint

All rights reserved. No part of this publication may be
reproduced, stored in a retrieval system or transmitted
in any form or by any means, electronic, mechanical,
photocopying, recording or otherwise, without prior
permission in writing from Fitzcarraldo Editions.
Without in any way limiting the author's exclusive
rights under copyright, any use of this publication
to 'train' generative artificial intelligence (AI) technologies
to generate text is expressly prohibited. The author
reserves all rights to license uses of this work for
generative AI training and development of machine
learning language models.

fitzcarraldoeditions.com

GOATSONG

PHOEBE GIANNISI

TRANSLATED BY
BRIAN SNEEDEN

CONTENTS

HOMERICA

(*Prelude*) 19
(*Episode I*) 22
(*Nostos I*) 23
(*Nostos II*) 24
(*Lotus-eaters I*) 25
(*Nostos III*) 28
(*Ithaka I*) 29
(*Lotus-eaters II*) 30
(*Nobody I*) 33
(*Achilles*) 35
(*Leukothea*) 37
(*Thetis*) 38
(*Penelope I*–am addicted to you) 40
(*Sirens I*) 41
(*Circe I*) 43
(*Peleus*) 44
(*Penelope II*) 45
(*Phaeakia*) 46
(*Ithaka II*) 47
(*Circe II*) 49
(*Nekyia I*) 50
(*Sirens II*) 51
(*The Ravenous*) 52
(*Episode III*) 53

(*Nostos V*) 54
(*Penelope III*) 55
(*Nostos VI*) 56
(*Episode IV*) 57
(*Nostos VII*) 58
(*Gift or Patroklos I*) 60
(*Penelope IV*) 61
(*Patroklos II*) 62
(*Aphrodite*) 64
(*Orpheus*) 66
(*Nausicaa I*) 68
(*Nauscaa II*) 69
(*Penelope V*) 70
(*Hermes*) 72
(*Eurydice*) 74
(*Nobody II*) 77
(*Exodus*) 79

CICADA

Ecdysis
    Leaves 87
    Birthday 88
    Weaving 90
    Whirring Cicada 91
    Cicadas 93
    The Present Moment 96
    Preparation 101
    Poppy 102
    Breath 103
    Rites of Passage 106
    Dream: Leda/Helen 108
    Phaleron 110

Winged
    You Me 113
    The End 114
    Rose Geranium 115
    Touch 116
    The Other 117
    John and Yoko 118

Earth and Sky
    Archilochus 121
    High Road Low Road 126
    Sublime Harmony 129

Depiction of an Original 131
Earth and Sky 132
Horse 135

Voicings
Fish 141
Word 142
Bed 143
Time 144
Places 145
Thought 146

Testimony
Eos and Tithonus 149
Tiresias 150
The Junk Dealer 153
The Car 154
Backyard 155
Homeless 156
Borrowed Brightness 157
Zeno's Paradox 158
Paros-Piraeus: Mini-History of the World 159
Via Egnatia 160
Platanidia 161
Stones 162
The Present Moment II 164
The Ferryman 165
Testimony 167

CHIMERA

the narrator says 174
Noon 175

1. DOGS 177
   Prelude: Gray March Sky 184

2. EARTH 187
   Noon 194
   Dusk 195
   Dusk 196
   Dusk 197

3. THE HERD 199
   Rumination 205
   Thanasis Koutinas transcribes a Vlach song 207
   Cyclops 208

4. UTENSILS 209
   Flutes 217
   Hymn to Swallow and Nightingale 218
   Sun and Night Stars 220

5. WORKS AND DAYS 221
   Morning Epilogue 228
   Morning Hot and Windless 230

6. CHIMERA 231
    Transhumance I 233
    Noon 238

7. SACRIFICE 239
    Transhumance II 244

8. EPILOGUE 247
    Darkness Again 248

    NOTES 253

HOMERICA

terrible fly
you connect excrement
with the face

(*Prelude*)

a stone on the seafloor white
rows of blue pebbles the face
above them in the water
the bobbing of the boat on the waves
the speed over the waves thrust of wind
we are flying
a lone seagull on a reef
a congregation of seagulls
endlessly cawing will
from time to time
grow silent
like cicadas
whose incessant drone cuts off
at the moment of calm in midday heat
when from inside a car the drone repeats
faster
and you have forgotten everything
you cannot remember
the *how*
and now you're forgetting the *what*
If only how was the recurrence of what
forgetting the moment is for you a medicine
against
the finality of sorrow
an unchartered place where your head is covered
you hear the singer of yourself
words of Nobody
journeyman wanderings

air sea mistakes irreversible gifts
counting
you know well that self is a series of events
but have you learned yet that series of *hows*
is the wind?

(*Episode I*)

> '...what shall I tell you first, what second, and what third?'
> — *The Odyssey*

a stone on the seafloor white
the face in the pebbles of the sea foam in the mouth
sand in the shoe the foot
and the pines in the sand the car in the shade
the stranger is sleeping on the beach by the pines he came from far away
he crossed continents he crossed seas
pebbles sand strolls and words
a grandfather talks about his grandson gathers seashells
from the stairwell the observatory scent of food
in the early boats they're already cooking dinner
in moonlight
in the middle of the night they arrived in the middle of the night
and climbed the hill
nameless
—although Nobody names everything
himself the wrong moment
or was it time—
noon the drone of insects
noon the heart in the hands
noon just barely touching you
next to the ivy down there the sea is steaming
on deck in the daytime seagulls
fly near enough to steal from our hands
and go
on deck at night the row of chairs humming
one on top of the other

wanderings temples ancients snows sun rains wind
naked dressed
Bassae Aegina Sounion
Heraion Aphaia Acropolis Haephaestion Karthaia Pelion
Pelion Perachora Karthaia
Anavyssos Isthmus Sepias Ptoion Karthaia
temple of Demeter temple of Artemis
temple of Apollo temple of Athena
temple of Hera temple of Poseidon
Vrauron at the sanctuary with the giant turtle
night the masts on the car
the hum of the sea
beneath the rocks on the sand covering the rocks
Salamina an exercise for memory an exercise for death
on the boat Trikeri on the boat Pagasitikos
Anavyssos
on the boat Aegean on the boat Saint Kyriaki
on the boat Mikro
Platanias national highway
calm hot sea a limping seagull drinking water
us leaning against the tree
beside the weeds
beside the small olive tree
beside the car
at nightfall looking down at the sea
music over the loudspeakers
down at the beach
a wave has washed up a woman's purse
stone chapel
among the offerings a photograph of a celebration
night the islands across and lights off the highway

trudging back and forth in seaweed trudging
back and forth
in the sand
facing the other standing
again and again over and over
even when the goal is the end
the cleanness of the stars haunts you
their repeating shine

(*Nostos I*)

for mama

—can one live with memories?
—one can
—can one live with memories without
wishing for a recurrence?
—I don't know
(I don't know how they do it those who grieve the loss of ones they
 truly loved
but nearly always they find a way
to bear it even when it seems impossible
or they couldn't survive
without the other without him but life
plays other tricks time never repeats itself
the body knits to the soul resists
in order to forget
it remembers to continue to live)

(*Nostos II*)

for a long time now I've noticed the weight
how to lighten it I don't know
by now the heart is so heavy it has sunk down into the abdomen
so the head is empty
how to raise the heart to the head I don't know
then of course there was winter
head empty heart low
the light yellow the sea calm
a tree tilts inside a wave
silence
buoys in the water
in the distance an airplane splits the sound barrier
at the dock two men are beating octopus
and the umbrellas cast shade only on the sand
last summer is finally gone
last summer is finally gone

(*Lotus-eaters I*)

> 'And those who ate the honeyed meat of the lotus
> no longer desired for return, or to bring back news
> but wanted only to remain with the others, the lotus-
> eaters, contented to pluck the fruit, to eat and forget.'
> —— *The Odyssey*

I'll stay here forever next to the sea
close to the dunes—
in the line endlessly written and rubbed out
by waves on the shore
I'll breathe in the smell of water
off the pier's decaying concrete
inhale the musk of the seagrass
and oil-green moss snagged on rocks
the small splash the wish of the wave
that closes sight with the veil of the mind
here the place of worship the homecoming
rows of olive trees motionless seagulls
solitary at the watchtower at the rock's edge
here the bend of the eternal recurrence submission
there in the calm the dolphin is swimming
and listening to the last voice
of a cicada up a tree

(*Nostos III*)

lightness lightness lightness
life is nostalgia for lightness
lightness of the air in spring
under the trees one afternoon
words glide sun shadows light
lightness of summer mornings
lightness in battle
when the limbs of Achilles the limbs
of heroes rise on their own volition
as though a god had put wings there
where force is unnecessary
there
where there's an abundance of force
force isn't the product of will
but sprouts effortless inside
the body
when the breath of oneself is the breath
of weather around the body
the hand glides across the water
carried by the boat
which itself is carried by another force
machines or the air we do not care
lightness of the fly susurrating
insect which ceaselessly
wanders rises falls walks
weightless as a caress
lightness of the air in spring
neither cold nor hot

the body expands and accepts
nothing disturbs it
only joy from the touch of
brazenly embracing
embracing without intention without purpose
nostalgia of lightnesses nostalgia
of Paradise
we call it Paradise
when
each of the seasons is spring
the air just such a temperature
with no gravity
you don't need to fly
its enough to imagine
you are outside
as if you were inside
the body moves on its own
immune to effort
limp
protracted stretched taut
reclining upright
the eyes look and see
are glad from what they see
they listen to what they see
smell the air
the air embraces
scents of grass of sea
the sound of cicadas
sometimes the air can be a little hot
and because it's hot it can be
a little dense I mean a little light

the soul stretches
can't recall
it is inside itself inside its own body
I try to walk and fly
I am a bird without flying
uphill is downhill
the car sprints
the outside enters through the windows
I turn my gaze and see
two sparrows
I turn my gaze again
the sparrows have flown off
I do not know how all these
birds fit in the sky
I know without needing to see them
when I look
they're no longer there
I was there too
I want to be there again
a breath for a small gift
a small now that does not last
it will stay will leave will be forgotten

(*Ithaka I*)

in front of the long table
—foreign dinner guests wine
your head shrouded—
listening with tears to the song
I hear you leaving becoming a stranger
a dream I had in front of the TV
your language does not belong to me
telling the story opening your mouth
the stranger wants to be sent back
with chests full of gifts
on a night like this one blindfolded
with a crew pulling at the oars
and the boat Sleep
before turning to stone will tie off
in beachsand
beside the spring
bee jars
the games of little girls
and the grotto
with its two doors
Fame and Forgetting
will accept him without a word
dressed in sheets between
silence and silence

(*Lotus-eaters II*)

I will stay here at the bend of the road at the curve
of the bay at the edge of the cape at the peak
of the high mountain the open arms of the sea
at the mouth of the river
I will stay here
the apples red the pears spilling with juice the tread
of our shoes unworn
you go barefoot in light clothes
at the end of summer but winter does not come
so you sit outside until dark
with the sounds of nightingales the lights coming on
before long tables small dinners of twilight
with night-moths drunken dinners
the medicine eaten
the medicine a flower
the medicine the medicine
forgetting
each moment a new beginning
which is I don't know where I come from I don't want to go back
medicine
it's always right now always right now

(*Nobody I*)

now
in a small village on a mountain
higher than the bell tower
the spire of its roof an extension of the mountain
calls to mind another bell tower
that big one the Notre Dame
with a nest of monsters under its roof
thousands of hours toiling workers hanging
from wooden scaffolds
—were they wooden I wonder?
—all the world's scaffolds are made of wood
raw material for building such as
stone such as dirt
yet wood is like the tree wood is
from the tree wood is more like ourselves they say
than stone than dirt
you must build a house with your own flesh
even if you
—and this was always known—
will die first and turn to dirt
before it does
the Jewish god thought to make you out of dirt
the Greek had other notions
from stone or from oak
people made from stone people made from tree
people clambering on top of wood from a tree
building carving the stone and from inside the stone
they strive to make the shapes which haunt

their minds
with tongues out legs splayed thorns
on the skin rivets in place of fingernails
after the people had carved them there
after they had caressed them
they wanted to come down again
and now as tourists at the church's bell towers
swarm
on photo excursions after waiting in lines
there where you'd never climbed
why didn't you ever climb up
to see the square from above to view the city
instead of going back into the church
again and again searching
through the red candles the deep pulse of the organ
the cold which pierces you in darkness the multi-colored glass
to understand
who are these locals who these believers
and lastly
who are you the stranger
but still I did not know
when I found myself someplace far away
that after I made it back
to the place I'd sailed from
I would carry this foreign church
of foreign believers
with me I would carry it
until
the church's staircase
never ascended
becomes my own

the wooden scaffold and stairwell and bell tower
and the shapes carved in stone
blackened over centuries
of rain which falls and falls and falls
will be who I am now

(*Achilles*)

> 'Nobody is my name: by Nobody I'm known
> to my mother, father, friends.'
> —— *The Odyssey*

the boat DREAM is for sale
the tugboat ACHILLES and the STARLET
facing each other gazing eye-to-eye
the PRINCE ABDUL AZIZ
from Jordan
no one saw put out to sea
with lights blazing at night
the palace tethered all year long
the king is not here
sixty-five men
ghosts of the harbor
govern it day and night washing
endlessly looking after the boat
and you over there
I see you I saw you and also today
mending nets in the big fishing boats
ten to each one
today Sunday day of rest before the full moon
housekeeping like me
bent over your purple needlework
listening to music on the transistor radio
each man a glass of tea a transistor
with needles you mend hunched
eyes bloodshot
sable men in wool pullovers

nobody here wears
mute underneath the overcast sky
and in rain
the men from Africa
said they knew only water
they were born in water
water sweet not salty I say pedaling my bike
water of the Nile Egyptian
and I say also
your hands are frozen solid
from the cold of this northern-to-you country of mine
fishing our waters
mending patiently each year
awaiting the hour
of return to Africa
when for a moment the fishing stops and the sailboats
pull up on shore
migratory birds swallows
back to their own water
their own women
in earthen homes along the river
though now I can ask
which is the land of the migrant
the There or the Here
the origin or the arrival
how can he embody the Name
who once was nobody

(*Leukothea*)

between wanting to fall asleep
and remaining awake
between telling everything
and remaining wordless
on the threshold of sleep the crest
the edge of the wave the breath
as it turns and pivots inward
after it's lifted inflated lifted
after it's inflated stretched spread out
to the point of time
constantly recalibrating changing
the speaking wave
before it has yet to turn inside out upside down
always both outside and inside
translucent unproclaimed powerful absolute
wave
translucent unyielding unproclaimed anonymous
wave
each wave the same wave
each wave a different wave
before it has yet to turn inside out upside down
before folding like the head
of an octopus when they kill it
a song which sings the roaring song
the song death the song come inside
the song Universe
a wave
between the unfolding and the rotation

between before and after
between the day the night the outside the inside the
foreign the ours
a spider weaving its web
before it finishes after it starts over again
and again the motions together with secretions
inching along announcing
approaching from behind
between sleep and rising
before the body after the day after the word
at the crest of the dream

(*Thetis*)

Thetis
the one who is placed
perhaps
always the one who places
also as we know the one
who refused to be assigned
to surrender to a man
becoming
fire wind water
tree chicken tiger
becoming
lion snake cuttlefish
until once on Cape Sepia the mortal
bound her tightly gripping
the prey in an unrelenting grasp and
devoured her in love
leaving behind only her white spine-bone
the bone of a cuttlefish on the beach
washed clean by the wave
Thetis is no longer there
she blows a megaphone from the depths
of the sea
a funnel a great conch shell echoes
words saying
"despite all the ink I sprayed
the man devoured me
me a goddess and he a mortal"
the warrior always returns dead

(*Penelope I*–am addicted to you)

she has a passion for the pool
each day in the pool up and down
the same circuit again and again
the pool keeps her alive
swimming in it sustains her
the continuous back and forth
the rhythmic breathing
synchronicity of the hands and legs
with the head
in out in out
of the water
the head
repeatedly enters and leaves
blows inside sucks in air outside
pauses a bit each time in the lane
tiles underneath the surface under
the light
the bodies of strangers menacing
with caps and flippers
the water suffused with chlorine
the sky over cypress trees
the pool keeps me alive
the continual song
counting
one two three four five
six seven eight nine fifteen
nineteen blows rotations
the song of counting the repetition

turns you to stone
yet the song of the pool saves
saves me from the knowledge
he does not love me

(*Sirens I*)

words are not things
words are living
breath *souffle* boat island "you"
you gave away I took
you took I gave away
the boat hangs like the light
from the ceiling
we dived under
lay down and slept
inside
I dipped my foot to tear the water
while the boat was running
I cast out and caught nothing
I cast out and caught fish
overnight stays sailing sea laughter
rites of passage

(*Circe I*)

for Barbara Köhler

'...and from within they heard the sweet voice of Circe
singing as she wove her immortal web, such handiwork,
so finely woven and delicate, a wonder even to the gods.'
— *The Odyssey*

on this long voyage
where the boat skips on the water
after you thought you'd found your destination
you didn't realize you'd fallen
into the invisible web of the sorceress
the sorceress braiding and braiding
and singing as she braids with the voice
while from far away
mesmerizing
you unspooled the path of meeting
and the meeting is of course immediate
faces bewildered
though the place teems with wild animals
the transfigured companions that is to say myself
you are the companion
whose passions are but previous passions
or those to come
you imagine that your boat is leaping
darting ecstatically in the beautiful vessel
yet from the depths the drowned beckon you
those seen only in dreams
in nightmares of descending

beckon you they take the shape
and even the voice
of women
but it is they and you are they also
they are the fish and they are the setting sun
and they are its laughter and its dawn
and they are each shape you meet
messenger of words
foreign messenger and your own
as the boat moves towards the new lover's
house
joy and happiness filling
the breast
ensnared by the voice
it will dislodge obliterate banish you
it will leave you nothing except
the hope at the bottom of a jar
as at night you return again and again
ungluing your gaze from her scent
the hope that whatever rises
the shipwrecks and the debris are just
the invisible doings of an imagination
like battles and journeys
and the always new extraordinary encounters

(*Peleus*)

Peleus
tugboat at harbor
beneath Mount Pelion
he is made of clay
a mortal
Peleus
a smokehouse in Pinakates
serves wild boar
he denies the goddess her transformation
from flesh dirt to ember flame
the mortal son to immortal
Peleus himself refuses Fire
out of envy
a brother-killer a fugitive after cutting out
the tongues
of the prey in order to count them
spends his sleeping hours on the mountain
dreaming of the grooved hooves of Centaurs
he'll wake up surrounded
he'll leap the fence at once
and look down from above
mountains seas islands
brushing his fingers across piano keys
happy to cry out
"I'm not alone
in the tavern men in chorus
are drinking and booming out songs
for you life
the women goddesses
murmur counting stitches"

(Penelope II)

the life of a woman has life
but you gods already knew that
a woman does not forget
her own war but exchanges
time for the moment just before
the wave she exchanges it for the moment inside
the wave she exchanges time for fabrics
ornaments song
each woman is a weaver
songstress
but out of nowhere the wave washes her up
onshore
naked
with no ornaments no weapons no voice
but fortunately just then
she has to get back
she has cooking to do

(*Phaeakia*)

arriving at the shore
a flock of laughing girls
greet the shipwrecked
lead him
to town through the countryside
passing cypress trees
like upright spears
out of reach
you bathe in the river
feral skin anointed with oil
from the plain you hear the echo of scythes
fields brimming with crops stream past
your truck
the harvest this year and last year and always
has been good
after your arrival
the abundant field will vanish
lukewarm rhythmic breaths
propel you to the city
touching down in the plaza
before the bats
return flying
to their stone abode
the floor paved in guano untrodden
hanging upside down
from the vaulted roof
the stranger is forgotten already
a beggar dressed in rags
begging food by the air vent of the metro
that's me and you

(*Ithaka II*)

passion
pain
I count and count
at dinner
when the table is set out
with food axes arrowheads
and your voice from inside the speakers
sings
"the gift of the bed
is not a gift"

(*Circe II*)

> '...she bewitched them when she gave them foul medicine.'
> —— *The Odyssey*

inside the pot
head bent over
she cooks
a column of steam rises
you can see it from the peak
shading your eyes with a hand
a column of steam her voice
sometimes she weaves sometimes she cooks
a column of steam and smoke
smoke from the hearth
steam from the pot in the hearth
scented steam of concoctions
that when drunk transform you into a terrifying sorceress
time
time is a terrifying medicine
each day is a terrifying medicine
it drips into the cauldron
the same juice
unaltered
the fear
of what will come
the stranger without eyes
only hands
time is a terrifying medicine
it cooks in the lentils
it boils with sacred laurel

it cooks in the same water
as the bathtub the sink the water
from the basin the water for the laundry
in front of the sea
so that you can pour it
on the salty always new pure
water the water of the sea
your time is the savagery of undying life

(Nekyia I)

I do not know why I went so far
I do not know why I was wounded
deeply in the heart
I walked I went out ahead
all that I did was pulled away
by the cadence of water
the force of the body
the lure of the body drives you to allow
drives you to fear
still deeper and deeper into fear
fear rage grace rage fear
enthralled by the Sirens' song
fear of the loss of the body
fear of the loss of the voice
drones helicopters fighter jets
in the sky
were flying playing violin
the windows shut
I lost the key again
the morning of my return
I want to greet
to bravely shut in time
a brave start
the roses the wind the heart the glass
"your forever shut eye"

(Sirens II)

a new car waits for us
la macchina e mia come let's go
for a ride
come climb aboard
the garden of miracles
one day consumed inside another
one miracle inside the next
come let's go in the water
into the depths to kiss
come into the car red brand new
let's go where you've never dreamed of going
there'll be other summers
everywhere I'll be your driver
on the wall lines of ants will march
insects will drone in the ivy
while rising from the sea ascending
powerful the full moon
we'll be climbing
the soft hillside across
with the bells
the sheep jostling
and now a silence
suddenly the wind stops
in the blue light of dusk
in the valley the word like a bell resounds
—my only word
I'd almost forgotten you—

(The Ravenous)

people rush through their lives
surrounded constantly by food
they gorge on music
the other
the light of the sunset
is right in front yet I cannot see it
out of gluttony impatience I gorge
out of fear
to catch up to time
to my children before they grow up
to keep up
to go swimming to go out to get a tan
to watch you to touch you to smell you
to guzzle you to forget you
to eat all the crumbs
so that birds
and alms
are a last excuse
for our abundance

(*Episode III*)

for Dimitris

let me peel two potatoes let me roll up my sleeves
in front of the sink
two potatoes the skins in a bag
your back's become crooked
whether you hurry or not
time catches up with you
dragging the boat half ashore
half still in the water
dragging it further up so it stays
anchored in pebbles
the heat of new summer
dries the skin
the son the friend me him
and afterwards we walked under the dunes
I thought I smelled frying fish
the motionless sun on the horizon
the sea at midday like olive oil
yet a breeze rising further inland
alters the image of summer
draws freshness from a distance
carries dreams the current ones
with the old and now forgotten
absolves the face with light
like you rinsing potatoes at the sink
onions potatoes carrots trash
fleshy lips white teeth
the trains come and go again and again

(*Nostos V*)

I'm here lying down
in front of the window
sprawled out upon the bed
eyes closed
suddenly I do not care
if he loves me
suddenly I'm somewhere else
like one time long ago
feet in the sand
a bird flying in the light
feet in the sand
a mat of reeds
someone else's dream old dream of another self
another time long ago
another I
another you a wind blows in the soul
nearby in the water
a September heat
last evening
after a cool
August morning
I'm not here anymore

(*Penelope III*)

for Eleonora

she worships her children
when they were little she'd take their plates
and finish their food
even now she eats the leftovers
and also
she puts on the clothes of her daughter who's taller than her
when they're soiled and left out in the basket for washing
she puts on the socks
and goes in them to work
she borrows the dirty clothes
perhaps she's trying to save money on the laundry
or does the charm work
only if
it retains from the body
the strongest
traces
of our secreted smells?

(*Nostos VI*)

the seagull takes the measurement of your wings
the sea calls you
but you do not want it
you ache
at its magnitude

(*Episode IV*)

we met inside a room
a wave shut the door
your eyes were blue
then green
yellow
hazel
no—we met outside
there was a rustle of pines
it was noon
no—we met
at night
night wakes us
our consolation is the sun

(*Nostos VII*)

we are walking
all that surrounds us is ancient
the stones
the sea the air the sun
the river—without water
the river—with water
the river is old
the reeds the trees
the sheep with blue eyes
us
your stomach your hands
your eyes your voice
as the moon
rises from the sea
again and again for the millionth time
the god watches overhead
two first creations

(*Gift or Patroklos I*)

everyone wants above all respect and honor
for what they are for what they deserve
I deserve honor I will not beg it from you
said Achilles to Agamemnon when he took back his geras
his honorary gift
he said also to Odysseus:
he's the one with authority but
I'm the better Achaean
don't think for a moment I'll bow my head
naturally Achilles said that the first
and only time that general
took from him his honor
and death
as heavy as that
was the price
I've suffered losses to my honor so many times already
public honor
not befitting a mistress
you said listen I'm doing you a favor
one afternoon
today
I was waiting for you
and I Patroklos
I'm speaking to you and I tell you
that you are ruthless Thetis is not your mother
from the sea and from the rocks
that gave birth to you
Achilles

come and eat a cuttlefish
at our table
but then I want you to fuck me the way I deserve

(*Penelope IV*)

if there wasn't old age then she wouldn't be afraid to lose you
losing the other isn't quite as terrible
as utter annihilation and loneliness
is telling lies again
of course one accepts everything
bit by bit he figures out
times change
the loss of union was there from the start
in union itself
loss of the other in coexistence
no one's the same before and now
you I
not because time passes and nothing remains
not because we're always seeking something new
but because then you
desired me
and I you
for epilogue a plate of food wine and silence

(*Patroklos II*)

is it that language follows longing
or is it longing
that's inspired by language?
because Achilles does not accept because you
once rushed to bear arms
Patroklos because
we must since that time rush to recite
the war does not cease at all
a hawk suspended in the sky
the sheep huddled
in the stockyards
you did not hear the airplanes
the washing machine spinning endlessly
and in the fire
the air laden from elsewhere
and singing in the pot
the thyme the savory rosemary
chamomile after being crushed by wheels

(*Aphrodite*)

I too have drunk
we often say at night
from this your glass Aphrodite I have drunk wine
drunk water but
mainly this
bitter medicine of oblivion they drink you most often
lovers of eros lovers of the absolute
plucking daisies even after all the hairs have whitened:
monotonous monologue of the daisy
the final petal answering *not*
—*he loves me—not*
bent over the newly cut bloom
stumbling we tear at the petals again two at a time
we do not see the road we keep plucking
—*he loves me—not*
perhaps in the rush a petal must've fallen
but even if *he loves me—he loves me not*
you said:
I am insatiable this love isn't enough
I want the other like when
you offer your heart in your hands
and in the light your voice comes
from deep within the earth like when
it presses out the ends of tiny jagged lines
chamomile roots
joinings of the earth with the racing white clouds
of late spring
take take

take
from deep within up to the sky I am yours
waiting in vain again for him to tell you
(in vain because
casually he scans the beach
for fresh masturbation material
the distant unknowable attraction
of an unexplored body)
in vain because
he has long since forgotten:
the ache of wanting
your soul as much
as your body
which is why the myths are short
"a god desired a mortal
he chased her he caught her
he fucked her got her knocked up
then when she fell in love with him
he forgot her"

(*Orpheus*)

tossed into now
with the momentum of yesterday and tomorrow you sing
voice
of spring
the air laden with fragrances
from elsewhere from here and what's to come
waiting to catch the sound of his approach
laden but light
as light but full
your head
flies and sings
washes up onshore with the waves
marks time for the oarsmen
who sing with him and row
while driving
the fish to foam-level the fish
to the pitch dark of the deep
dolphins
lions deer beasts of the field
listen transfixed
in the afternoon sun
the gypsy shuts off the megaphone
brown-soil red-soil he shouts
soil for all your balconies
and circles back to sell
while in the dusk
a warm breeze carries
the dizzying fragrance of "angelica" flowers

he thinks of Eurydice his own angelica
lying with his own soil held tightly in his arms
and sings without pause
knowing that when he stops
he won't be able to keep from turning his head
to look on the past
and lose
him and her and the spring sun
and the coming summer most beautiful of them all

(*Nausicaa I*)

> 'Once in Delos near the altar of Apollo I saw such a thing,
> a just-sprouting young shoot of a palm tree.'
> —— *The Odyssey*

the Japanese poet Bashō had a banana tree
for a house and a name
the Greek planted another
in his garden
without metaphysics
he needed to feed his child

another Greek—this one Achaean—
met on a riverbank
near an estuary to the sea a maiden palm tree
I know only the palm tree of Delos sprouting from the earth
a bloom such as you leaves me in awe
—so he told her—
poor Nausicaa
he never even touched your knees
those delicate words heard once
only afterwards to lose forever
this supplicant laying at your feet
the owner
of the sunken cargo ship
it was—who else—your beloved father
who boldly drove the stranger out beyond
from where neither the boat that sent him
nor he would return
because he was going far—to where his longing was

for men longing is their destination
far from Nausicaa
so forget the stranger's honeyed words
a momentary balm for the heart
balm arrow to open the wound
it will never happen again
the stamp of the deed the indelible mark
though you still go on wondering:
was it better to have met him?
couldn't ignorance of happiness be
a mortal's shield?

(*Nausicaa II*)

what words did you whisper
from the floor of your navel
falsely
and the voice
and the glint of heat
from your eyes and hands
I should have been burned
I should have left behind only
my smell
on the things and words
on the sound of the earth spinning
night and day
night and day
on the axis of its solitary column
"I love you—forever—yours"

(*Penelope V*)

when a child is born
tenderness flows
like milk from the nipples
the sky clear
as its eyes that see clouded
something large born in something so small
open and closed
each newborn a Zeus in his grotto
suckling milk from the goat
powerless and therefore
mightiest of all
ready
in its hands the entire world
I woke in the night
to whisper my love for it
its struggle its strength for life
its socks its clothes
our own invincible scent
its quiet sleep
again a boundless gift has fallen from the stars

(*Hermes*)

> '... and Hermes led them through the shade of the mountains,
> the reverberating glades and blossoming fields.'
> —— *The Homeric Hymn to Hermes*

did you see me I wonder
as I swam in the sea
from above
as you flew in the sky?

you took off your sandals and wore woven leaves
of sea tamarisk
beneath the mountains of Pieria
to throw them off your trail O infant
a trail of theft and song
to the river Alfeios
you drove the herd with backward hooves
the stolen oxen inscribed the ground
tidbits to appease the table the assets of gods and poets
across unreaped fields and mountainsides
but you were spotted
while tumbling
from their airplane the gods
saw your bizarre script
among the scrub the scents of harvest time
gifts in exchange for poems
thieves poets singers without food
the fields still have a voice
writing to be read from the heights
of the mountains

of the heavens
the winding script of the machines

(*Eurydice*)

for Isabela M.

'the poison of immortality brings the passion of women to a close.'
—— Marina Tsvetaeva

shadow dream
how pointless this struggle
since it's not about victory
since you struggle beyond expiration and oblivion
perpetually to protect
to not forget perhaps to repeat
to hold for as long as you can hold on
to swim in the sea again
at the axis of the world
at the moment
and the point
between the setting of the sun
and the rising of the moon
you want to go back from Hades
you a mortal
I turned back to look and I was dust
I turned to look and I had been forgotten
I turned back and my children
big now the young plants
like two sprouts had shot up
while
those I didn't give birth to
irrevocably never

will not come into being
as slowly fading each and every summer
yourself
only visible now in the mirror
becomes that other
who also fades away

(*Nobody II*)

in memory of Pierre Vidal-Naquet

coming back years later
having forgotten the names of the streets
of course you still remember the way
the body knows where to turn how to move
to get to the front of the building
from the stairs of the metro the escalators
the place empty
no beloved
the notebook with its phone numbers lost
thrown out with the rest during the move
quietly now you count the dead until you
are recorded among them
it's raining like it did then
you're thinking again of Pierre's ruined necktie
at lunch
on the way to lessons the request for an escort
at the entrance to the library with the question "who"
qui va m'accompagner jusqu'à Jussieu
the short walk to the station and then to the metro
gripping the handles a few words the assault on Iraq
and you still remember mixed with and surrounding these
the darkness of rain the sadness without cause
the aimless walks
aimless walks with no thirst
and no quenching
only joy this talking with Pierre
laughter filled with intelligence with sarcasm the barbs of love

knife against bone to test how much you can take
because you must learn you must
know how to answer
who you are and why
he wants to toughen you and with it wants to know
if indeed you can if indeed this
is truth to you
and now
years after he's gone away as
alone you return though you've lost the habit
the place has become strange again
and even more
there isn't even a reason
the reason is people
those you avoided leaving and those you found
by going
you can only remember
fragments of familiar places and fragments
of meaningless moments
but most of all yourself
this particular self talking with Pierre
this toughening of volition
in the place where it always rains
far from the sea
how you planted the oar in the earth
how suddenly you realized what the reason was
for coming back
and to carry it back with you
in order to give birth
and be able
to bury

and be able
once more for the last time
to love from the beginning

(*Exodus*)

for years
until yesterday
I was a girl
it took much of my life to become a woman
it was very hard for me to grow up
now I say that I am
woman and girl together
I've won them both
they are mine
I'll be an old woman and I'll be the only one who doesn't know it

CICADA

'Quickly the shedding progressed. Now, the head is free. The proboscis. Now the front legs gradually emerge from their casings. The body suspended in a horizontal position, legs upwards. Wings fledgling. Still creased, they look like the curved indentions of an arc. Ten minutes are sufficient for this first phase of transformation.'
— Jean-Henri Fabre, *La Cigale: La Transformation*

'SOCRATES: ... as we know, cicadas were human once, but after the Muses invented song some people were so entranced by the pleasure of singing that they didn't eat or drink, and before they knew it, died.'
— Plato, *Phaedrus*

'Stillness
the cicada's cry
drills into the rock'
— Bashō, tr. Robert Hass

Ecdysis

Leaves

Inside these articulations
the beginnings of language
outside of yes and no
inside only the I want
the soul with the body meeting
in all the openly
meteoric leaves
and now, see:
one of them falls slowly
to the earth

Birthday

Do the wings itch as they sprout?
When from the exit of the abdomen
you first raised your head
and pushing from the pain
sprang into the light
to cry out
were your eyes open?
Did you listen to their words
as they held, gently
your contorted body
gathered, legs tucked
and the day warm?
A woman giving birth
on the floor of her car—
is each growth
painful as the first?
Doesn't one grow
at the same pulse, imperceptibly?
Or is it after periods of stasis
when motion seizes you suddenly
and you grow and are unbearably changed?
Do you cast off the old
like the flower its petals
in the dew that you suck,
again and again?
Inhabited
by night's afflictions,
do you open your morning eyes
slantwise to survey the world?
You've gathered the stars, you hold them
in your hands, you scatter them
onto the earth and the sand
taller than ever,

you the tree
we fit inside your tiny shadow
lighter now, lighter

Weaving

The word by itself germinates
exists
beyond our decision for silence
every creature
on its path to the other
sings
but the threads of the planets
are distinct
no matter how closely they are woven
stutterings of half-raveled words
that though written
never mean what they say
or even what
you thought you meant to say

Whirring Cicada

I.

Only the voice desires
sweet voice thin as honey thick
dribbles and spills onto the earth below
Tithonus in his cage
whirring cicadas
the milk thistle flowers
as the burning state within a state
of summer detains each of us
the blaring cicada spills onto the ground
the voice
of the one who ceaselessly desires
and recites
from his own cadence relentlessly dizzying
like sirens drawing us imperceptibly to sleep

II.

Cosmic monotonous song of the cicada
each person according to their own mind
receives another melody and tone

Cicadas

I. Archilochus

Leaves of ivy play with the wind
apples redden on the branches
and then fall
the mouth fills with words
cicadas
blend with the noise of the cement mixer
and the ants
that walk along the wall
cutting a path entire armies
walking single file
to our dinner table
pears in the basket
you've spread out to ripen
you talk about partners
and the shield you tossed
into the game
say you were bravely defeated
through the ivy the sea
beckons you
distant bewildered turbulent

II. Winged words

for Mitsos

From drums in the viscera
a cicada screams
song of gathering
marked by weather fluctuations
and the dance of the other male
chant of premarital rituals
song of annoyances
croak of protest in captivity
when you catch its wing
seized a cicada by the wing
the summer my brother
ate a cicada
it fluttered
and screeched
alien voice from the fence
of the teeth
when the mouth opened
the cicada
took off flying

they call you cicada
you always face the sea

III.

The coming of age
we hope it will leave behind our voice
voice greater than life
because as Socrates says
cicadas
attendants to the muses
did nothing but sing
ceaselessly
to die in the end
fam-
ished
singing with the authority of an empty stomach

in Aetolia today the children will tie the cicadas with a string and then leave them on a branch to hear them sing

(though in captivity
they die)

The Present Moment

I.

The wind carrying the voices
cools ruffles sleeves
travels to the edge of the dress
while over the asphalt
in front of the wheels
sparrow dances with the butterfly

II.

I open my mouth to speak
but my teeth clench
you a seashell
a hidden word
buried in the seabed
a mollusk
motionless in sand
with its antennae
twitching towards me

III.

Because the moment is inconceivable
not present at all
the "present"
"that which is here"
space in place of time
the tongue speaks in absence

IV.

Because meaning in language elides
my words
the baton
a pebble
borrowed
indefinitely they resemble another presence
before me
opening a path
and when the path is stepped on again
it is mine
and it is not
and when the path is stepped on again
it becomes a pit
to fall into

V.

For the hand that writes
the words
a voice speaks
shares assigns
bearing the thing that is most yours
even if it is borrowed
shares time
in fragments
shares prolongs
beyond all of us
stepping well and high
feet up in rhythm
music
towards the other
opening
towards the sun
pure longing
within absence
Apollonian dance

at the pier the moon
refuses its turn to come out

Preparation

Only then was I living
in the absolute present
while also preparing
the present
which belongs to preparation
I mean to the building of
each brick that is added
one by one
absolute now
before it stops
as
the sound of children's feet
racing
and the briskness of the doors'
opening and closing
the absolute present
for us
is the preparation
for them
of desire
and crickets have camped out
under the roof of the schoolhouse
perched in front of the microphone
to magnify their voices
and they serenade us
from their nook—
it's gone
it's gone
it's gone
what you were waiting for passed
without your noticing
it was already raining
raining
raining

Poppy

When from a distance and within
the body opens like the petals of a flower
as when the poppy bends
weightless head from the inexpressible
there are no rooms then
doors couldn't open
or even shut
see then
it whispers to itself
see the time Eros chose to take me
in the flowering sea
in the deep dark

Breath

I.

Breath of wind you blow and come
on the balconies at night as we sit outside
gazing at the sky
flowers trellising
a light whiff
as the butterfly flickers its wings
and standing on a flower
bees
suck juices make love
with their mouths and feet
sucking what's beneath
and the shifting weather
because who's to say
who can categorize elsewhere
in his collection
elsewhere the butterflies
the bees and plants
elsewhere the cats the goats
or the trees
elsewhere the mouth elsewhere the semen
elsewhere the stamen and vulvas
breath of wind
you who gently caress faces bodies
gradually naked
tossed into unshuttered night
with the sky's dome above the earth
wedged open
and in the joining we
slipped ourselves into their entwining
creatures of summer
sensually seeking a sweetness

and taking in
through the pores of our skin
open passages connecting outside and inside
pathways to the mind the heart
memory
all of us
tiny transmitters and receivers
in the great funnel
of the universe
spiraling endlessly
breath of wind breeze of the sea
voice whispering
I say take me
in your embrace
in your violence
and gently
let me go

II.

On summer afternoons
the soul's smoke
climbs and disperses into the previous
from other years
an accurate memory
waiting to be burned
inside the next
on this same day—August 20th
recalling
the heat the sweat
our cool respite in the water
in the now to be touched
in the eternal recurrence
of rebirth
plane trees lean down to the water
the crickets giant grasshoppers
organs of abundance
night
the stars
wading in the sky
each year
our vain return
to witness

Rites of Passage

I.

How do we go from one season—to another
one hour—to the next
slow and torturous and continuous
hence the rites of passage
all the ache
mixed with
all the fear
severing before from after

II.

You were crying—the clothes you wore
as a child
which constrained you
and which you'd been forced
to part with in order to
afterwards
in your new body
fall in love

Dream: Leda/Helen

I.

From a single egg
she waits
to be born
—she says—
without knowing what it means
because she was already born
because she had given birth also
first she would crack the shell
—she says—
into fragments
to break the membrane
and then you
o daughter would spring out
most beautiful of beauties
like every daughter
you'd emerge from the egg
to enjoy again the same pleasures
to make again the same mistakes

II.

You birthed the egg and you were the egg also
ripe flesh in spring
mumbling lullabies
for you and your daughter
how protracted and hard it is
to grow
to go from a child to a woman
to fly like a swan grieving
its former life

Phaleron

Afternoons my mother
would feed me
on the sands of Neo Phaleron
next to us the trawlers were leaving to fish
—what's a trawler really?
is it a boat that fishes with a net?
all that we can name by knowing and
all we name without knowing
language
blind
it catches them with its net on the seafloor
brings to light
fish mollusks oysters seaweed junk
with no name
within the person who grows up watching
the sea before them vanish
and the pile of debris that hides
the horizon
and the island across the way

Winged

You Me

You giving me without asking giving me because you want to give without even knowing you give giving me effortlessly when I never expect it but also perhaps when I do and when I expect without knowing it or your giving this knowing before I do in my place wanting what I want before I realize I want it or wanting what I want because you are more me than I am wanting together the same thing or wanting what the other will give us when they give it giving together before we can think of it or want it and for it to be a shared desire or to be ready to receive it to have desire in place of the other when you tell me we're going to do this I know you'll like it and we do it and I like it more than I thought I would maybe I like it more because you thought of it and not me but you thought of it on my behalf before I could you were me before I was myself because the two together are something else that goes further than our separate I's a double me a double you

The End

I wonder what'll become of us in the end the end for both of us what we are now what can words say about it I don't know the words I don't know what words say words that we say aren't ours the words for us don't belong to us the words spoken are always foreign often I think the end has come though you're close to me your body feels foreign no I mean your body isn't foreign but your soul is different somehow not mine I know how it feels when it's mine when I recall it I think perhaps the god has loosened the knot and tears begin to seep down to the eyes I stop them when they touch the brim I stop them because you're here even though I want you to know I'm crying for the end because I hope the end isn't real but an idea a moment of unfaithfulness between one and two between myself and you still I want you to prove it to me and since nothing has been spoken I return everything to its place again I begin to wonder again I recall again how it was I found again how things might be I remember that paradise existed in the infinite of the sea under the vastness of the sky one facing the other and one's eyes in the other's eyes one's body in the other's body the other's soul in their body and in their soul though everyone knows how first creations end

Rose Geranium

A plant in a pot a pot beside a table a table with chairs with people a plant in a pot in front of a road followed by sand a beach then sea the plant is green intense green I don't know the names of the green when you cut it and rub it between your fingers the plant has a smell its smell is intense I can't describe it smells and colors are never described except in metaphors the plant is used in sweets for its aromatic properties down the street people walking the sounds of forks and knives laughter conversations the sea crashing on the beach spraying the plant in the earth beside the steps beside another aromatic plant named *verveine* we call it *louiza* in Greek the French also drink it in a tea like chamomile a sedative at night I drank it also before sleeping when I decided I'd be tranquil always but then chose the agitation the ecstasy in life the ego that ricochets within the body the body within the world naked filled with emotions mutable yet always the tranquility returns it returns so we can live we die continuously until at last we become eternally tranquil

Touch

Where's the cell phone did we bring it you asked and began to look through the bag the bag that was always filled with stuff filled with everything in disarray tangled up with one thing inside another with your arm deep inside the hole you rummaged the dark sanctorium I think it's in here you said though I'm not sure because I just barely touched it if it was really what I was looking for and so we continued on our way why should what you touched not be what you're searching for I said what you touched and didn't see is always what you search for you have to trust your touch as much as your vision I said maybe even more I thought touch and smell are closer to memory closer to truth because they're nearer to the body than vision to smell to touch I have to be in close contact one on top of the other only one on top of the other the truth

The Other

I looked at the photograph many times I look at it often and also the other photographs from back then your face our faces back then the faces of other owners the faces of other people is it because it was a different time I asked it's because it's the past you said it's because then was then I said then with someone else you weren't the you I know you said I look again at the photograph the gaze is different the laughter more open the gaze more tender I say to myself the world for you was lighter then and the eyes you were looking into weren't mine I said you're kneeling the angle is from above you're smiling calmly with joy with the sea behind you used to belong somewhere else I belong somewhere else I'm unrecognizable a stranger you said men don't enjoy looking at old photographs women like it I said they're always looking to find what will hurt they're always looking to find what will hurt not only in what will happen but also what happened what happened is far away from us now you said and yet it's not it's always near I said what happened is gone but may return the stranger may come back again inside the one you love the hidden stranger a ghost waiting to rise to the surface to take on another gaze another laughter turning to face someone else and you become him and I'm not her

John and Yoko

Lying face up in bed that photo of John Lennon and Yoko Ono the one taken from above do you remember ten years ago in that other house that other time it was still the same position the ceiling looking down at us what does one ceiling see that the other doesn't if only for a moment we could be each one from its particular point of view different from the outside from the inside two identical snapshots ten years apart two snapshots with two different pairs one of John alone looking at Yoko from above and the other of Yoko with the same John ageless immortal dead and she alive mortal older looking into the mirror of a photograph over millions of years couples intertwined lying face up couples facing the ceiling the sky and lying there

Earth and Sky

Archilochus

In one of his books, Athenaeus preserves
a verse by Archilochus that goes like this:

"As for the figs of Paros—famously
called *aimonia* by the locals—Archilochus
commemorates them with this line:
ἔα Πάρον καὶ σῦκα κεῖνα καὶ θαλάσσιον βίον."

ea Paron kai sika keina kai thalassion bion

In English: *goodbye to Paros and those figs and life on the sea*
Eight salvaged words, preserved by choice:
Someone (Athenaeus) wanted to commemorate someone else
        (Archilochus)
who in turn commemorates something (the figs).
The objective of this preservation is memory, the opposite of forgetting.
Through writing, what one knows and retains
is preserved.
And so this verse passes to our hands.
Eight words of alliterating *k*'s and *a*'s.

The first word: *ea*
In English:
goodbye
And now back to Greek
say goodbye to it—to Paros
calling to mind of course the last line of Cavafy's poem
"The God Abandons Antony":
and say farewell to it, the Alexandria slipping away from you.

And though the first word in the verse that sets the tone—*ea*, an
    imperative—
was translated *goodbye* in English

really it's more like
"I leave I abdicate I omit I defy I relinquish I
abandon I ignore I neglect." *Leave it*—then—*Paros
and those figs and life on the sea*
or even
abandon it, Paros.

The same word, *ea*,
is said by Odysseus to Achilles
ἀλλ' ἔτι καὶ νῦν παύε', ἔα δὲ χόλον θυμαλγέα
i.e.
"stop now and abandon
this rage which injures your heart."

ea, the second person imperative of *eao*
brings us directly to the question:
who is speaking, and who are they speaking to?
Someone (we guess the poet) addresses
in the second person imperative
someone else who is leaving Paros
or must leave it
and telling them to say goodbye to it, to leave it, to abandon it.
And the other could also be the poet
(a monologue then: "abandon it" to oneself)
or even the reader, I mean, us.
And maybe the imperative can be taken to mean the inversion
of a particular situation:
"leave it (the place where you now live)"
and maybe it also conveys
acceptance,
acceptance of finality,
acceptance of the inevitable to come.

ea: the first word, which sets the fragment's tone
abandon it, it doesn't fit you
or on the contrary

say goodbye to it even though you don't want to
say goodbye to it because you must.

Second word: *Paron*
That which must be abandoned is the island, Paros.

Third word, also the sixth: *kai*
A connective conjunction. It joins with Paros,
with those figs, and with the life on the sea.
Used twice it also means: not only, but.

ea Paron kai sika

Fourth word: *sika*
Fig: fruit of the fig tree
but also, fig: female genitalia, according to my dictionary,
or as Aristophanes put it:
his fig thick and stout
where hers is sweet

ea Paron kai sika keina

Fifth word: *keina*
keinos: poetic Ionian version of the demonstrative pronoun
ekeinos
Demonstrative pronoun demonstrating a person or thing
far away in place or time
yet already mentioned.
Not just: the figs
but those figs *there*, not here.

From far away the speaker
POINTS AT THEM WITH HIS MIND,
like Vamvakaris when he sings
"of the Creator"
and points at god

far away and not here.
Those figs, with emphasis on *those*, those far away,
aren't here anymore
those you can gaze upon from far away,
those you remember, nostalgic already,
or those that have passed, or the reverse:
those you didn't want, which afflicted you,
those goddamn figs over there.
Together with the first word, *ea*,
the fifth word *keina*
restores emphatically the tone and tinge
through its *e* and *a*.

ea Paron kai sika keina kai thalassion

Seventh word: *thalassion*
thalassios: adjective, meaning "of the sea."

ea Paron kai sika keina kai thalassion bion

Eighth word: *bion*
bios: life, the way of a life.

Bios thalassios is the life of the sea,
the life next to or in or along the sea,
the life bearing characteristics of the sea,
the way in which one lives in the sea,
or the manner in which it provides food.

The fragment's diverging interpretations
arise from the rich tone and tinge,
whether the figs are vaginas—an erotic life corresponding
to life on the sea, gladness—or suffering or exhaustion,
or the figs are being eaten,
and the edible fruit of late summer is associated
with life on the sea as

food, seafood, and fish.

We are free
to choose our own interpretation every moment,
for this verse that causes us
to go away and leave
because the second person imperative can always
mean us
—in the open fields of Paros,
sea and land,
paradise or affliction, in August.

ea Paron kai sika keina kai thalassion bion

Always an admission, a salutation, of *those*.
Say goodbye to it, to Paros, not only to its figs but to life on the sea.
Abandon it, Paros, and those figs and life on the sea
Abandon it, Paros, with its figs and life on the sea
Abandon it, Paros, with its loves and its life along the sea
Abandon it, Paros, figs, and sea
Leave it, Paros, and those vaginas, and the afflictions of the sea
And say goodbye to it, Paros, and those figs and life on the sea

Or, better yet:

ἔα Πάρον καὶ σῦκα κεῖνα καὶ θαλάσσιον βίον

High Road Low Road

I.

For partnership between equals
pairings of opposing powers
male female
sky earth
north south
cold warm
up down
light dark
right left
Heraclitus answered:
high roads and low roads are the same

High roads and low roads are the same
not in the sense
as I once thought
that the exhaustion of going uphill and downhill are the same
but rather
that uphill and downhill are accorded the same value
ascent and descent
good and evil
if made into an equation
$+(\alpha) = -(\alpha)$
male equals the opposite of female
with equal absolute value
add them together and you get 0
or even
from that same unit
two split fragments
one's curve matching the other's
so that when joined
we'd have a perfect sphere—with the crack

Aristophanes mentioned
of the two severed from the beginning
and through Eros
perfectly fitted again

here is the sphere
made from two halves
if you consider it in terms of composition
the sign of the Tao is completed
two joined without division
and should it appear like antithesis
we have Strife
semiosis difference limitation
war
the strong onto the weak

II.

Instead of making opposites be equal Empedocles
preferred to complicate the union
and perfect assembly
of two parts
and the intertwined
members roots plants animals
and from their union to originate
a plethora of composite disparate data
deviant blends of cyborg creatures
Empedocles's addition doesn't end in subtraction
no invisible glue
from each joint something Other
goes missing
something entirely different
a surplus of subplots and array

Sublime Harmony

"And the white bones exquisitely dovetailed
by the glue of Harmony"
naturally Empedocles
with a name like *everlasting glory*
the glory
rubbed off on the ground
where we stand
and so on
speaking for the white bones
which somewhere along the way Harmony "dovetailed exquisitely"
he must have come across
the white skeleton
of a perfect Being still in its joints
Exposed and Polished by the elements
a Being Older and Stranger
or some Being he knew well
in both its living form
and the one it retained
after death cleaned it to completion

(he was crazy about free will
Empedocles
with his feet rooted in "glory"
meanwhile of course
Heraclitus
was bored to tears
because while the other
labored tirelessly
to set up his construct of variations
painstakingly he
Hera's glory
in a single sentence delivered
each time

his erudition
condensed
contentious
ironic
dark
the Dark Truth requires a Clenched Ass)

Depiction of an Original

One
simple
to be described
yet distinct
and were you to add
one to one
once more an original one will come out
1+1=1
each time another child
distinct
the same complexity
simple
to be described
words say something less
and something more
hair blond brunet curly eyes blue brown
strong knees spread arms

Earth and Sky

I.

Clouds have enveloped the mountain
losing its peak in the sky
which like an embroidered dress
covers everything
encircling with its body
the body of the earth
humming ceaselessly
and us mortals below
with friendship joy
joining limbs
like our works when we look upon them
and when they are complete

Strife stands apart
parting one into many

II.

Sky dark
sea gray blue
trees acquiescing to gusts of wind
everything obeys the sky
bowing, rooted to the earth
only a ship in motion
has volition to resist
a machine's volition
invisible to us
propels it onward
life is that which leaves
motion volition
forward
what parts the volition of others
from the sky?
what parts it
from its roots in the earth?

III.

Is the departure
the journey
just a working
of sky?

if fate is the sky
one which
comes from somewhere overhead
one which
like war or earthquakes
finds you.
The name of the unknown was always Sky.

Horse

I.

Starts to prepare to begin to uproot
the invisible rungs of the ladder
spiraling into the sky
they close their eyes for a moment
breaths drawing in the double dance

are they singing now?
or perhaps dancing?
traveling
galloping in emptiness
in the desert's vast
empty spinning infinite?
on what road?
galloping over what?
is one the other's horse?
or rather
is one the top and the other the bottom
as they ride mounted
on the same horse-
body
to carry them at this speed?
only seemingly governed by its rider
when it's they who belong to it
it steps on the ground and runs
while the deluded
with their digits dangling
in the air
forgo spurs or saddles

thought action shifting from here
to there to here following

limbs perceiving motion
fingers edges openings mouths
surfaces
signs
whatever it seeks it finds through touch
the mind's focus leaps frenzied
from one here to the other
joining here there here there there there

open
to what touches
closed eyes
open to see
then closed open closed
when they open perhaps they encounter
the face
when they open they encounter
another's eyes, yours
perhaps they peer into their depths
gaze piercing the soul
to the bottom to find only emptiness?
on their road
do double gazes
meet?
or is it that they encounter
the other's contact
with the infinite far away?
now a pause
the gathering of powers the onset
of a wind damp but not chill
the air of winter caressing
the sky weighted with clouds
from the quiet gray sea
swollen
the soft earth anticipating
it rests

the sound of the roll of the waves
the sound of the beyond
the beyond over there
touches the flesh the skin
in the kitchen a pot is boiling

II.

in stillness Hannah says only in stillness
can a human think
only in stillness can a human accept the world.
ἀναπολῶ: I invert revert return
going over it again I reiterate
I invert the earth with the plow I plow
I revolve in spirit I meditate consider:
when the soul in itself reminisces
when the soul reminisces itself inside itself
this I do in stillness
as our steadfast horse
reminisces about the tender grass tufted from earth
and with the plow of my mind I dig and dig
the soil
I dig to recover some old roof tile some old song
that grew before my stepping here before me
I kept it in a drawer
when they tried to take it from me I hid it deeper
when the soul inverts the soil of itself
inside itself
when the soul inverts
the soil inside it
rare double root
you inhaled
air and light

Voicings

Fish

Wherever I stand I see the sea the sea facing the window the sea through the mirror facing the window the sea in the clouds in the sky the same as the sky in the sea a bird a seagull flies and leaves the sea through the window of the mountain the mountain through the sea in the sea beneath the sea in the surface of the sea behind the sea beyond the sea the earth's sweat the sky's teardrop inside the boat beneath the boat and along the horizon's curve the sea the horizon inside the fish I eat but the fish never noticed doesn't know the sea doesn't know the horizon always present inside the sea the fish doesn't have a balcony

Word

From my house I look out at the sea existence is a thing of places places in the world physical and otherwise places with and without others the intangible places the places in this world are stable they have a latitude and longitude they have a given width and height they have geography when I cease to exist I don't have a place anymore they say the words *I* and *here* come from the same root yet the place of memory persists even Achilles Best of the Achaeans dies and is left to remain without his death his place only temporary yet with his death it perpetuates it becomes permanent our place only lasts in the memory that exists after us but how can memory exist without the knowledge of the one I met that one is able to remember me remember my body my voice more mine than how I appear and afterwards when the one who knew me is lost in turn I'll be lost too everyone is lost after death with the death of friends only a sort of biological continuation persists through time a nameless immortality

Bed

How do we give a funeral for this animal how do we bury it after having lost it never to be found again we loved it it was there next to us in the house sometimes it sighed sometimes it farted it was an animal cinnamon-colored with brown eyes it looked at us sad its tail wagged sometimes the animal wanted to go for a walk it looked to the fireplace it laid its braided head on its front paws the animal was female in its psyche there was a butterfly with heavy wings and in its psyche it read our own reddish animal cinnamon-colored it took part in battles it took part in sorrows it took part in joys meals dinner conversations always together as we grew up so much that we forgot it so much that we grew even older so much and before that we also shook the petals and before that we died it was a dog her name was Daphne

Time

Our connection to others is the time we give them said the man in the movie when he was about to die or maybe he said the time we give is all we've got I don't recall exactly maybe he could've also said that time is the only thing that exists nothing but time said the dying man and then you start realizing how little time you gave here or there and maybe when you were or weren't giving that time you realized the same thing differently I mean the meaning of presence and the meaning of absence we always say it's distance that matters and not closeness distance that creates desire whereas closeness erases your desire and my desire this is one way yet one could argue another way if the intensity of my presence and your presence can be equalized if time is not just a quantity but an intensity though time is defined by quantity what is a mortal's time but the quantity of their existence this countable time of a mortal's lifespan is mortality this lifetime of closeness and distance time apart and time together is all that's given to us spending our procession through the world is only this wasting of time time which without knowing its final quota arriving from elsewhere is given to be mindlessly spent

Places

—Yet there are things we do not decide said the man who was about to die meaning of course his own death—but you can't die said the woman who loved him there must be something we can do let's go to America she said—there's nothing to be done he told her and with this knowledge the knowledge of his death which is equal to the knowledge of our nonexistence our nonexistence between the constant existences of others and automatically equal to being forgotten and automatically equal to our own replacement by other persons other persons everywhere and in every possible place persons replace without actually replacing because each person is singular this being the definition of person yet even still the replacement exists maybe it's the replacement of the role I mean the replacement of the place that is mine yet someone else's yet still my person no one else's and with that knowledge the protagonist selects in the arrogance of despair his own replacement his replacement in all the places that he once occupied and who he believes won't be able to replace him in the end because he still believes he's superior we always believe we're better than our replacements

Thought

Death doesn't exist says Epicurus because while we live we're alive and don't know what death is and later when we die we don't exist anymore so death doesn't exist for us he said this because he knew that we know we are going to die and this makes us different from other animals his words and thought are valid because of course if animals possessed thought they'd be in our position too because they'd have knowledge of the future thought means projection projection means changing one's place in time or in space according to Nietzsche the joy of animals is tied to lack of memory and so the present is only the present meanwhile a human sees the present through the past alone yet also sees the past through the future I wonder can a human see the present through the present what does it mean for a human this moment where she lives this hour where she lives it's already been forgotten this moment this now was only ever from the outset irrevocably dead

Testimony

Eos and Tithonus

It was Eos who prayed
for Tithonus—a mortal—not to die
begging that his days become
numerous
as the grains of sand emptying from her hand
and the Sibyl asked the same
to Apollo, yet—
now they seek their own ghosts
in the pauses
between grains of sand
in the bodies they embrace
eyes closed
seeking in vain
a single drop
—Nightingale and Cicada

Tiresias

I.

Lying in the sand
a snake
licks my face
behind so many eyelids
eyelids of silence
I glide from creation's
slightest crackle
the cloud's chasing
the tree's shedding
the thought's shimmering
the wave's scintillation

II.

Oars:
boat's wings

III.

Rose with the thousand eyelids
pomegranate
with the thousand seeds

IV.

Cicada eaten by ants

V.

Houses by the sea
light air of September
distant noise of the saw
garden shadows
a woman in black sweeping the road
pomegranates, plane tree, cypress
angelica
a man with a dog
underneath the olive trees
sofas cast-iron chairs
from the '60s and '70s
backyards of vacation houses
wealth within so little
gravel, flatbread, and pines
nostalgia with black wings
crosses from beyond the sea

The Junk Dealer

"Kitchens washing machines old fridges
old storage units I'll empty"
the junk dealer who buys words I wonder
will he buy the light?
(the words are coins
the water scrubs them
to polish them
so they'll shine as they fall)
yes, he bought the light
a dime
and goes about singing
proclaiming the same and the same
binding past with future
brimming with longing
and they clang
inside the old jalopy
the pieces of scrap the old lamp's skeleton
the spring

The Car

We got rid of the old car
that for so long had born us in its viscera
like an animal
a sagacious donkey
it accepted us it ferried us unharmed
observing our squabbles our kisses
our children growing up
now when they unload scrap
at the ports
from the old cars made in china
our mouths clogged
we inhale the motes
of our own rust

Backyard

From the backyard facing the mountain
pra-pra pra-pra pra-pra
the engine of a boat
conveys the sea into the room
like warmth into the bedsheets
a body
missing a while now

Homeless

In the morning in the room
we found a bird fluttering
confined
with the window open
it kept speeding up to fly
and hitting the ceiling

nests
the homeless homes of birds
each with its own sky
each with its own freedom

Borrowed Brightness

> 'Lit with a borrowed brightness, wandering the earth'
> —Parmenides

I can't see her
she's hidden herself
light suffuses the sky
like night's zipper left open
filtered blue over the mountain
a man hears
but doesn't listen
even to his own voice
touching the edge of the universe
shoulders broad
eyes full
of glaucous deep blue gray light you
sky
you rinse us
not knowing our fleetingness
whatever you let drop appears new
inside the radiant ancientness
the man hears
the woman opens her palm with its blueprints
far from thought
wind caresses the houses
filtered blue brightens the expanse
eternal moment of gaze
without purpose

Zeno's Paradox

Night
where blue horses of the moon
graze
where the roaring
of the vast flower of the sea
opens one by one its thousand petals
where in stillness the distant
murmur of the mechanical crane
echoes unloading from ships
containers of sand for making cement
you wait
you bite your lips curl your tongue
you have no voice
you wait to come again to find yourself
and go back to the beginning
mortals
so that you may leave
up on the highest branch of the tree
your apple
there where nobody
neither your hands
nor the insatiable mouth of time
can ever reach

Paros-Piraeus: Mini-History of the World

On reliefs inside the large graves
you can observe in fine detail
how they caught ducks with huge nets on the Nile
how they drove water to the fields with sluices
how they swam in the water by kicking their feet
how they ate onion bread at the table with their hands
how the cook would cut
vegetables into slices with his knife
and fry the onions in a pan
how the mothers would call out at dusk
to draw their children home
how giant magnolia flowers would fall suddenly
slowly white on the dirt
how the cicadas stubbornly kept singing
even after sunset
how the sea was calm at morning and restless by noon
his fingers struck the keys so violently
the crickets reminded us
of this late summer
that soon ends

Via Egnatia

—What did you see and what brought you sudden pain?
which was the stabbing knife?
—the glued-together heads of the lovers
drinking the other's mouth
with no quenching
a bridge
suspended over the valley
Arachthos
far from the wheels
water leaks from everywhere
the sky
the roof of our bus
licks, wets the mountains
each bend a new rivulet of mud
and another tunnel
beyond the curb
alone
traveling
the pain in freedom—the unknown destination
over an abyss—the foreign teenager
clinging to the back of the seat
outside, two houses gently touch
shoulder to spine, pressing
like sheep
trees signal
the presence of the ravine

Platanidia

Were you to pass fallen leaves
on the road you'd see
waves licking
women in pairs on the benches
from the courtyard where a table overlooks the sea
you'll see men lined up to fish
tearing off on old mopeds *pra-pra*
fathoming the sea with rods
(though she gives them little)
leisurely the men
only pretend to work
waiting like the rest of us
for the unexpected to appear
a red fishing boat
coloring the wave
I walk along the shore
among the scent
of bitter mud
mud of the field mud of the seabed
scent of evening primrose
soaked yard
yelping dog
a waiter with a tray
crosses the street
a solitary woman
a cricket
I have no secrets from you
which is why I'll invent
a stone filled with feeling
a sea still as a lake
a sky

Stones

I.

I wanted to be able
to become a stone
a mute stone deprived of language
and each night
bereft clear-voiced bereaving
for years each night singing
until all feeling drained out
and exhausted I burrowed
into the dreams
of the youth who grieve for the future

II.

Our dream gathered
and spit us out polished
in the night
without tears
without the depth of touch
the morning couldn't find space
to bring its light
across to the other side
on the riverbank stones
one by one
open their eyes

The Present Moment II

And sudden
as the eye catches
a bird in flight
flitting darting
something alights

suddenly and discovers you
the absolute present
that which finds you
without your asking
the unexpected

and shortly afterwards or perhaps
simultaneously the desire
to shake off to step out
into the future
to seek something undiscovered

to repeat the unrepeatable
nostalgia
the first sensation that immerses
each creature
after it leaves to be born

The Ferryman

I.

You saw the ferryman
alone
slicing silently
the sea
leaving behind as he slices
that which always remains open
what does he see as he calmly progresses
towards the outside
he hears
the sky
shimmering
in the inexpressible light of water
what does he see
the mortal
he rehearses at death
wind
the absolute horizon
only the leaves of the olive tree know
what lies inside him
—a rehearsal in light

II.

Rehearse in light
person human mortal
within what floats
cast out for your shadow in the faraway mountains
so small or so large
as you progress unmoving
you imagine you've abolished it
while on solid ground
from where you can be seen
the sound of wheels
relentlessly treading
the stones even as they roll
lightly on the soil
deeply rooted in absolute dark
ferryman sealed inside a shell
we're yours
"better to be eaten by fish than by worms"

Testimony

You, cicada
you don't exist anymore
I'm coming to find you
I'm combing the tamarisks
the sea exhales
from wind
a plastic bag hanging
from the branches
you, cicada
you don't exist anymore
the black eyes of summer
are closing their eyelids

CHIMERA

χίμαιρ-α
chimera, *f.*

I. she-goat, sacrificed before the battle to the goddess Artemis; wild goat; young female goat; a kid.
II. *a.* legendary fire-breathing creature with the body of a she-goat, the head of a lion, and the tail of a dragon.
    b. name of a volcano in the Cragus Mountains of Lycia.
III. in modern Greek, a metonym for a fantastical creature, a vain daydream, an unfulfilled desire, a utopia, a self-deception.
IV. in modern Greek, a botanical term, a graft, what is made from joining a rootstock and scion.

'Since the end of the twentieth century, our age, a legendary age, we're all chimeras, theoretical and created hybrids from machine and organism; in short, we're all cyborgs.'
—— Donna Haraway, *A Cyborg Manifesto*

Microchimerism (Mc) refers to an individual hosting a small number of cells or DNA that come from a different individual. It was first observed in humans when cells containing the male Y chromosome were found in the blood of women after giving birth. Being genetically male, the cells couldn't belong to the women bearing them, so it was assumed they originated in the embryos during pregnancy. In a recent study, however, scientists noticed that the microchimeric cells in some women didn't just circulate in the blood, but also integrated for several years inside the brain. The prevalence, diversity, and durability of the naturally obtained Mc in healthy individuals shows that a change must be made in the conventional way of thinking of the self as individual, to one that conceptualizes the self as a chimera composed of many parts.
—— from various online sources

The poem, then, is a speech for two (*Gespräch*, joint-speech), a speech for more than one, a speech that contains more than one inside it, a speech that collects more than one "I."
—— Jacques Derrida

ΧΑΊΡΕ ΖΩΟΝ

HELLO ANIMAL*

* Welcome-screen message on one of the narrator's first mobile phones, Nokia series (circa 2000). Animal: ζώον (*zoon*), from life (ζωή, *zoe*), creature, living thing.

the narrator says:
goatfold of Yannis Mourtos in Kalamaki Larissa.
750 stock, 700 females. goats.

two winters I went among the fold with Chara
I saw the animals scream and fuck
                (when the human let them)
I saw the animals being born
                (with the help of the human)
I saw the animals graze
                (led by the human)
animals shorn and adorned
                (when the human wanted it)
I saw the animals slaughtered and skinned
separated from their mothers.
Life and death together
determined
by the human that does unto them
as a god.

Noon

a row of cypresses towered over the road
we knelt at the water's source
drank its cleanness.
plane trees shaded the ground. shaded
the brown-on-brown tufts. wool from shearing
residue of hands on the bodies of animals.
at Easter the ditchwater purples
while in the square, huddled together, awaiting
sacrifice, the chosen offering
bleats.
flesh
prey for humans
shared with wine.
wine blood. wine bread.
dirt.
'A soul dressed in a body,' Empedocles says,
earth surrounding the mortal
earth surrounding the death-susceptible
earth surrounding the already gone.

1. DOGS

Narrator: How many dogs have you got in your herd? There's what, 700 goats?

Uncle Yannis: Mine? 13 dogs.

Pouqueville says:
The dogs that belong to the Vlach shepherds are Molossian hounds, fearless, eyes lit with a kind of fire, their pricked ears catching even the slightest sound, vigilant sentinels, friends of the hearth, the family, their masters for whom they would give everything. They step proudly at the front of the herd, which they contain without even once showing their fangs. They contain the land, watchful of wolves, which they attack, and they nearly always emerge victorious.

> *Goatself:*
> to learn about the goats
> I spoke with the shepherd.
> he belonged to a nomadic people.
> spring on the mountain
> fall in the valley.
> he was a seaman,
> when he retired he came back
> to the herd.
> he was strict
> he cursed politicians.
> I asked him for his dog
> he said not a chance.
> there was no way
> he'd ever
> give it to me.

William Martin Leake says:
The shepherds of Kipinas would sometimes graft a fragment of bone from a dog's foot, about two inches long, into the side of a grown sheep. They would open up the flesh, place the bone in, and sew up the wound. This procedure had two benefits: it fortified the stamina of the sheep for the mountain's harsh weather, and it also callused the flesh, imparting a foul smell that repelled wolves.

> *Goatself:*
> to learn about the goats

> I took from the shepherd
> his dog.
> now it lives with me in the city.
> it's good with strangers
> though sometimes it can be
> a little aggressive.
> but out of affection
> because I am both
> the shepherd that feeds it
> and the goat
> it must guard.

Edward Daniel Clarke says:
In East Katerini I met a group of Arnaut shepherds armed with large pistols and knives. It was strange to us, how they clothed their sheepdogs to keep them from the cold.

> *Goatself:*
> you said I am your goat
> and you are my dog.

the narrator asks:
how old is it?

shepherd:
one
a little acorn this
just a pup. We tossed it in with the goats to know them,
see how it plays, how it paws the dirt.

> *narrator:*
> hay clinging to its back
> eyes laughing
> rolling on the dirt floor of the pen
> curling up
> with baby goats in its arms.

Yannis Tsevrechos says:
I emptied my rucksack, and what food I had I offered to one of my cousin's dogs I found watching over two newborn kids. Throughout the night it laid curled so the goats could nestle against its belly.

> *Goatself:*
> caring for another saves you
> from your dominant self.

Yannis Tsevrechos says:
Their feeding time is before the herd is let out to graze and after they come back. At the day's start and close, the dog is the first and last concern.

> *the narrator says:*
> for centuries they fed the dogs
> black bread made from bran. not yeast.
> and in the same basin where
> they kneaded the dogbread
> women gave birth
> if a baby came during
> the walking season.

Giorgos the biologist says:
dogs and wolves
are classified under the same genus
—they used to list them separately, nature/civilization—
those that could digest starch
the humans took with them
to eat bread—like them.

Leonidas the historian says:
wolves worship the strong
the breed bows its head
hence domestication.

dialogue between the shepherd and narrator:
— That dog took on a bear up the mountain,
got his tendon torn up. That's why he limps.
— What's his name?
— Davelis. Like the bandit. A warrior. Yet he's the
quietest one. Just lies around.

Dimitris Loukopoulos the folklorist says:
somewhere out there the sheepdog
opens and closes its eyes.
and the shepherd farther off
in the thick shade of a fir tree or perhaps a cedar
lying on his belly or his back, depending on the moods of sleep
drinks the polished air of ridge
and wood.

> *Goatself:*
> I'm accompanied by
> that most yours
> and delicate
> first voice.
> I'm accompanied by your breath.

Loukopoulos says:
in the deepest shade
the shepherd sleeps
on his back
the dog sleeps
everywhere, a solitude and stillness.

> *Goatself:*
> always it comes
> following behind—to sleep beside me
> to place
> its head on my thigh

       thigh—head
       a new double animal
       companioned.

Homer says, the translators struggling:
ἀπόθεστος
δὴ τότε κεῖτ' ἀπόθεστος (εκ του θέσσασθαι)
and so he laid there scorned
and unseen, no one called for him
ἀποιχομένοιο ἄνακτος
and when his master was away
he lay unseen and scorned
before the palace door
where the shit of mules and oxen
streamed endlessly

ἔνθα κύων κεῖτ' Ἄργος, ἐνίπλειος κυνοραιστέων
Argos the dog laid there, covered in ticks
he who, when he sensed Odysseus approaching,
wagged his tail, lowered his ears
though he lacked the strength to rise and go to him
and Odysseus, seeing him, dried secretly
a tear, and entered straightaway
into the palace.

              Goatself:
              Argos
              from the word *argos*, meaning swift
              in Homer's time, now it means slow
              the Swift becomes slow
              the dog once royal—now a beggar
              on the steps of the palace—
              through some insight he knew
              he too
              had taken the guise of his master
              and into a beggar

>   had changed
> or maybe it was his master
> who chose to enter the house
> in the guise of a dog?

the translators:
Ἄργον δ' αὖ κατὰ μοῖρ' ἔλαβεν μέλανος θανάτοιο, αὐτίκ' ἰδόντ'
Ὀδυσῆα ἐεικοστῷ ἐνιαυτῷ.
and after twenty years of waiting for Odysseus
and finally laying eyes on him, death seized Argos.

> *Goatself:*
> waiting by the door
> for years, until he'd grown old, until
> he was prepared to die
> waiting, and when his master came
> no one
> but he recognized,
> the dog and slave who
> on seeing him wagged
> his tail, tried to stand
> and let his soul out
> with its small heart
> which had for so long
> companied.

Prelude: Gray March Sky

Each spring I give again the burial of myself.
I bury the others, the previous springs
I bury this spring, which is not like the rest
I bury myself in spring
so that I may crawl inside my body in summer
and tear from the desiccated hide of autumn
and winter, stubbornly, to insist the ghost
of my compulsion
winter would have absolute freedom
existence in the vast expanse
of Mongolian highlands, the gallop
of long-haired horses, the words
of singers from another season, storytellers
but—
as when at the end of winter, in the fatigue and exhaustion
of daily regimen
a star flashes suddenly in the sky
of the cup of wine we are drinking
in solitude together
and the star's glint leading us astray
down old paths, driving us to open once more
we owe this opening, the paths nearly closed
from branches and ferns
we owe this abandonment
again and again each year we bury
what we were and leave behind
an exoskeleton of singular form
each different but multiple
we bury it with ritual in the grasses
we leave it in the bright stems
of weeds it clung to, we rip it out
we bury it in the sand, we toss it in the sea
on the way we meet women carrying bouquets

of wildflowers, gazing off. Slowly
and tortuously we begin to clear the paths
there in the middle space of the half-opened
beneath the earth, in myriad creatures
spring is sleeping.

2. EARTH

Yannis Mourtos, owner of the herd, shepherd ever since he was a boy: This one time, guys, we had a place in Grevena. It was so muddy that if we got caught in the rain, our shoes would peel off. The ground was heavy clay, and if it was raining you were stuck. When we made it to Kalirachi the next morning, the women would say, "Sleep well?" "Shut up." Why? Because of all the mud!

X: The mud was very sticky.

X2: And what kind of shoes were you wearing again?

YM: What kind of shoes. Pig-tsarouchia! Pork-leather.

Yannis Mourtos shares a proverb:
what the goat does to the holly, the holly does to the goat
or
what the goat inflicts on the holly shrub will be told on the
    goat's skin
meaning
what you do to others will happen to you.

The tanner says:
goats are tough, they eat hollies.
but the hollies are barbed, which scrapes their skin
and leaves cuts and gouges we find later
when the goat is processed
in other words
the skin is a canvas, the skin is earth.

William Martin Leake says:
Those villages mostly get by making a rough woolen fabric called *skouti* that is then used to created overcoats, called *kappais—cappe* in Italian—worn widely in Greece and the Adriatic. The fabric is of two colors: white and black, and the inner part is a coarse wool sent to Venice and Trieste in lengths called masts.

Panagiotis the cheese maker says:
my *yaya* used to weave, she had a loom
we threw away a few years ago
because no one used it anymore.

narrator:
                    in this place

                    the earth's surface

a carpet woven

                    from human animals

humanimals

the carpet of earth

eternally woven
        for time to tear apart

timeweather tears apart what humans animals weave

        time and animals within the ground

the weave of man

        undone.

Panagiotis the cheese maker says:
my *yaya* was tall and thin but very strong
could shake out the heavy wool carpets by herself
after washing, like it was nothing. When she was widowed
she climbed the mountain by herself
with the herd and the children too.

the narrator says:
the goats eat: oak, acorn, strawberry tree, grass, broom,
Cornelian cherry, blackthorn, wool, dog rose, thorn apple, pear,
wild vines, firs.

Makis M., former breeder, says:
I knew a shepherd once who went foraging on the mountain and ate
by accident the berries of a belladonna, so-called because women in
Europe put drops made from it in their eyes, to dilate their pupils, so
their gaze was more intense. He stumbled down the mountain with
his axe. Tried to kill his children. But they dragged him to a hospital
and tied him up, and for a full day he whistled and called out, poor
man, for his goats and dogs.

Goatself:
hours by myself
I dream
leaping here and there
I choose a branch
and chew
branch by branch
step by step.
I choose the sky.

Pouqueville says:
The herds descend the mountain's slope in undulating lines, one can see the clatter of their hooves and hear their bells—the *tsokani* bells of male goats, the *trokani* bells of the females, the rams, and the sheep—in miraculous harmony.

Makis M., former breeder, says:
Another time there was what we call a *gisemi*, a castrated ram, and they gave it a large bell to make noise with, we called it the *tuba*, it made this metallic jingling sound, it was spring and they were going up to the pastures, and the brush was so thick you could hardly hear the smaller bells, and if a goat ran off into the thicket even two hundred yards away, it was lost forever. But if you had one of those bells on it, the sound travels, a huge echo, penetrating, and you can follow where it goes, so they would put it on the *gisemi* in spring to help them find it. It's their GPS.

William Martin Leake says:
On its south side, from where we entered, the town ends at a precipitous cliff, close enough to the opposite side on the ridge that voices could be heard across from the church there, the Agios Georgios. As if this is the first surveillance transmitted when travelers or caravans come from Ioannina... It's a strange thing, how much the communication owes to telelalia, to speaking from a distance. It's an art, like *telescopia*, which is recognizing things that are far away, something the Albanians and mountain-dwelling Greeks have refined.

Goatself:
the pillow:
I made a mountain
and fell on it to sleep.

A Vlach song, sung by girls, goes:
Where will we stay tonight?
Behind the sea
a caravan passes
laden with salt
and a grand young man
on a horse
with his elegant combed hair
and waxen mustache.

Iris says:
eros. agape.
love.

the breeder says:
And a goat that had left the herd during the night came over and right there two meters away it says "baaah baaah." He was on his period. Testosterone. "That" was what it sought. It made these cries from deep within. Like those of a bear, guttural—a bear's growls. That's what the goat was looking for. Its sounds came from inside.

Goatself:
you carry everywhere your own
piece of dark
the skin of your living blood
silent
shredded in stillness
pillow
dreamtank
drips of poison
within the body

        unseen
        ἀεὶ πολεῖ.

the other song goes:
the girl from the east and the boy from the west,
two strangers, met in a strange place.
"You're a stranger and I'm a stranger,
come, let us spend the night together."

        Goatself:
        me I was born
        of the sea.
        they stuffed my mouth
        with earth
        from the mountain.

you:
you're beautiful
like that.
like a goat

        perched
        on top of me.

        Goatself:
        I'm the goat
        you're the mountain slope.

Matsi:
goats are rocks come to life.

        Goatself:
        a laughing wave.

narrator:
are they any different:

rocks of the mountain
and rocks of the sea?
the same shepherd scales them.

Noon

from a distance we could hear the wild galloping
of hooves on asphalt. we turned our heads
struggling to see through the trees. then
after we got onto the freeway
they overtook us. violent joy
reddened their faces. steam rising
from their strong bodies running.
in their purple beadwork.
their proud straight tails. their vast inexplicable
eyes. for a brief moment I manage
a glimpse of their thighs shining moving.
holding deep inside them
the sun. for the third time midsummer
unfolded red roses at our house.
sometimes I can't stand the thought of what
waits for me.
let it come let the unexpected
find me. a wind.
no one will be able to say with words
where it passes.
a scent.

Dusk

walking in the woods in summer we came upon
loggers. we heard them before we saw them
before we saw them we came upon their traces
walls of logs stacked by the side
of the road waiting for transport
freshly cut trees.
and the bare patch where their bundles
bundles of lithe, young chestnut trees
left behind clearings following their slaughter
before we saw them we heard their voices. distant
and esoteric in the expanse of the shaded wood
why too this sound of bells?
ringing as they climbed the ravine
and turned onto the road
then a rustling of leaves in the low branches
hooves. voice
and you passed like lightning out in front
first the neck glinting with blue talismans
the four black feet and last
the bright eyes of your flaxen head
a second horse hauled lumber. riderless
then the Centaur was lost
in the black wood's thicket
our dog followed them at a distance before turning back
you can only follow a dream so far.

Dusk

for Maria and Andreas

a bald spot on the mountain high up.
warmed by the sun before dusk.
as I enter the clearing a young fox
jumps to its feet and runs off
sheltering in mountain ferns.
blueberries are ripe. I wrest a few
from the horse and plop them in
my mouth two at a time. each has its own
flavor. even those that grow side by side.
one more sour. more sweet. bittersweet.
near the sea we found koumara berries.
on the beach beneath the trees
sleep. contentment's incense
weighs our eyelids.
stay with me Oneiros stay
don't leave me with Hypnos alone
I want to fly with you a while tonight
over lands over waters
mountains. seas.

Dusk

I saw the farrier as he was finishing up
the last horseshoe on his knees beneath the horse
filing
with its left hind leg over his shoulder.
he wore a leather apron. he was handsome.
then he gathered his tools and devices
and climbed into the truck. his dog next to him barely a hand-length.
in the shop the saddle maker
with axe and adze works
the goatskin lays out the skeleton with trinkets
floor submersed in straw. torn saddles littering
a string of lilting consonants from his mouth
bird's beak. cadenced mountain-speak
when he talks on his cell phone I understand nothing
leading astray the mule drivers and the shepherds
the belled saddles of the animals
bear the burden. always
singing ensconced.

3. THE HERD

Uncle Yannis: Because there's love there for humans. Because I lived with them, so, I love them. Ask anyone in this line of work. It's a hard trade, this. I don't know. Ask me anything about breeding, and I can tell you. Anything! There's nothing. 'Cause since my birth, since I started, I was in it. When I climbed up on the horse, the goats came over, all seven hundred of them. When it got dark and I made a fire, the goats would gather round. There's no science to these things. Don't need one. The science of veterinary medicine is death.

X (a goatherd): No science. Only practice. Practice teaches.

Andreas Moukas, from Mt. Parnassus, says:
to call the goats in the morning, we shout: *hei hei hei, tou tou tou
    tou, tsoi, iou prts, hei hei*
and to get them out the pen we call: *hei hei hei, p p p p,*
    (whistling with his fingers), *pr pr pr pr, fr fr fr fr, k k k k,
    hei hei hei, tso, tr tr, ye-he-he-he*
and when we want them to back off: *ha pro tsoi ts ts ts tso*
when it's time to feed them salt: *tsoup tsoup tsoup tsoup, pr tsoi,
    pr tsoi, ts tsoi, he he-he-hei, hei hei tsoi, pr tsoi*
to gather them: *he-he-he-he-he yo-he-he-he ts ts tso he-he he hei hei,
    strou strou, stro strou stro tsp tsp tsp tsp (whistling with his
    fingers), hei hei hei*
and to bring them from the pen for milking: *ts ts tsoi.*

Derrida says:
The herd isn't simply a society of animals, the herd is a set of grouped animals, domesticated animals, monitored and controlled and intended for consumption. I've just spoken about domestication, about indoctrination, about appropriation, about the transformation into pets, but there's also livestock; the herd is a group of animals raised with the purpose of being used and consumed by humans.

the shepherd names the herd and its inventory:
shepherded herds:
herd (*kopi*, meaning cut)
herd (*nomi*, meaning pasture, law)
horde (*ordi*, meaning swarm, gang)
herd (*kouradi*, meaning shit, sheared)
lamb herd (*arnokopi*)
lamb herd, ages two and up (*zigourokopi*)
ram herd (*kriarokopi*)
goat herd (*traoukopi*)
herd of females with no milk (*tsagkadokopado*)
herd of females with milk and their nursing young (*galarokopado*)
ageli, goat herd, *gidokopi*, little sheep herd
miliorokopi, goat herd of firstborns

specifically goat herds:
katsikia goats and *katsikakia* kids
garbage herd
tsaggades childless mother herd
male *sirko* and male *arseniko*
the early goats *proimadi*
late-born *psimadi* and way-late the latest
vetoulakia little weanlings,
herd of childless goats between the ages of one and two
        weighing over thirty pounds
milioraki, the one-year-old *vetouli*
unfucked *milona sterfomiliora* birthless
little *tragaki*, the two-year-old ramlet

trai the three-year-old ramling
males' ages are measured with scissors
from one, two, three snips
mounochia, dickless ram
castrated ones, *katsikomonacha*
neutergoat *kopania*
marmara the sterile one
pratara impossible to separate from the sheep
herdfollower
zavatariko sly one and scourer.

Yannis Tsevrechos says:
often the very intelligence of the animal,
of the herd,
doesn't let you make mistakes.

Dimitris Loukopoulos says:
Goats can be a naughty bunch.
Protected by the Devil, they say,
when the goatherd is away.
So you see, what can a goatherd be but another Devil?
It's difficult, you know, to change the mind of a goat.
No other animal is so destructive.
If one takes a branch in its mouth, good luck.
If one happens upon a wheat field, it turns it into a threshing floor.
They'll climb into branches and make mincemeat of the trees.
They'll climb onto the shingles and turn them to Swiss cheese.
Always when goats pass through, it's a biblical event.

The General State Archives mention:
All Vlachs and Sarakatsanis should be dispersed to faraway provinces because each of them, without exception, views theft as noble and will hide criminals and vouch for alibis, and because each is connected through family ties to wanted thieves, each has racial sympathies, and it's considered a virtue to harbor criminals.

Some proverbs on goats (Loukopoulos again):
A wise man never lets a goat guard his vineyard.

If a donkey eats a vineyard, it will grow back. If a goat eats a vineyard, it won't grow back. The goat has a venomous tooth.

The goat devours everything. It's because Christ cursed it when the goatherd refused him water.

The goat later betrayed Jesus to the Jews when he hid among the herd and they lifted their forelegs and revealed him.

The General State Archives mention:
Their herds should be collected and confined to each village, or else they should be forced to build sheepfolds near one another, within earshot, so that the barking of the dogs of one pen can be heard by other shepherds close by, because they are known to hide thieves out of fear or self-interest.

Terminology of the Vlachs, Giorgis Exarchos says:
Kouanta di entou
Kid's-tail, referring to those who are arrogant and aloof—a kid's tail always sticks upwards.
Hi toutipouti
(unknown)
mou katsikothike, to overstay, to get one's goat
katsikokleftis, petty-goat-thief.

The General State Archives mention:
Thus all tent-dwellers without exception—Sarakatsanis, Vlachs, Gramoustianis—should be required to camp near established villages in order to be monitored by soldiers stationed there, because should they camp far away from the villages, they'll have no qualms hiding thieves, supplying them with gunpowder, new shoes (*tsarouchia*), and whatever else they might need.

She narrates:

    Goat:
    female animal of such-and-such genus
    after learning her hooves
    after weaning
    she ruminates her food
    recalls it back into her mouth
    from the stomach to consider it again.

(Become a goat before you speak, my mother said.)

    ravages everything
    in her path
    used for clearing
    unusable fields
    unwanted
    ungovernable
    unsuppressed
    free to climb where she wants
    to leap
    she plows all the earth with her feet
    in heat and thirst crying out.

Giorgos Giannisis the biologist says:
In all ruminants, the upper incisors are missing. So the jaw has adapted, resulting in a kind of callus (*tiloma*) in the upper part. Similarly the lips and tongue have adapted in order to gather the grass and bring it into the mouth. A characteristic all species share is the rumination of food. They gather it with their tongue or lips, cup it with their incisors, they chew it slightly and then swallow. At which point it enters the larger stomach occupying three quarters of the digestive system. There the food, once fermented, enters the reticulum, where it is separated into small bites and returned to the mouth again where it is chewed, or ruminated, and mixed with saliva. Lastly it is swallowed directly into the omasum, where digestion is completed. This process of rumination isn't one that ruminants learn the day they're born. Rather it begins the

moment they take their first food aside from milk.

the narrator says:
from the moment of separation
from the mother
they ruminate.

Rumination

within me words voiced
like dictation
when you dictate
and find the starting place
grasp the thread
and the flow begins
words following words
to speak then hesitate
catching it again
correcting it
smoothing it out
or making it even more feral
for effect
shaping it again
you ruminate
and all this voiced
loudly
up and down the room
and the next word comes
an image emerges
flashing before the eyes
then feeling
singular
to that moment
all of it is woven
and you want to say it
with words appropriate
in value to what was given you
and these are voiced
again taking shape and meaning
until the road runs out
rewilded
our steps bewildered

our decisions obsolete
until the trees the roots the branches
the buildings
seal the path
the faucet
stops
!

Thanasis Koutinas transcribes a Vlach song:

Namisa si aceĺi doi muntsî	Between two mountains
Elu moi ana moi anamesa oreeee	He that goes between
Iara ună fântănă arace	There was a cold spring
Elu moi ana moi anamesa oreeee	He that goes between
Iara djone pliguitu	A young man with a wound
Elu moi ana moi anamesa oreeee	He that goes between
Tu tămpări avărtitu	Wrapped in a cape
Elu moi ana moi anamesa oreeee	He that goes between
Stu părnari arucutitu	You birds that sing
Elu moi ana moi anamesa oreeee	He that goes between
Puiĺi tutsî lu virgărară	In the fallen holly tree
Elu moi ana moi anamesa oreeee	He that goes between
Voi lăi puĺi ci achiuratsî	All the birds enclose him
Elu moi ana moi anamesa oreeee	He that goes between
Tutu întregu s' nu mi măcatsî	Don't eat me completely

Elu moi ana moi anamesa oreeee	He that goes between
Măna îndreapta s' ńi alăsatsî	Leave behind my right hand
Elu moi ana moi anamesa oreeee	He that goes between
Ta s' ǵrăpsestu 'nă lai di carte	To write a black letter
Elu moi ana moi anamesa oreeee	He that goes between
Ta s' pitrecu la dada s' tate	For my mother and father
Elu moi ana moi anamesa oreeee	He that goes between
Ta s' mi plăngă ta s' mi jiĺastă	So they know to mourn
Elu moi ana moi anamesa oreeee	He that goes between

Cyclops

I'm locked inside the cave of the Cyclops
with his solitary eye guarding me
I stay awake.
— Cyclops open the door for me!
— Cyclops let me leave!
the Cyclops caresses the fuzz on my back.
lights a fire
rubs his hands
eats my meat my cheese my wine
sleeps happily
still guarding me
burps
with his solitary eye open.

4. UTENSILS

Uncle Yannis: The goat wants it. I mean, really needs it, you know. It likes it. It's a comfort: the bell, all of it. Humans are the same way. We're no different.

Yannis Mavrakakis: The *kolevda* was a small satchel made from the shaved and sometimes tanned skin of the testicles and used by the shepherd as a cup for scooping water from the well or tank, and sometimes for drinking milk after milking, or filling from the milk jug. This and the *fouska* (bladder of a slaughtered animal) our shepherds used for holding tobacco.

Jakob Johann von Uexküll says:
The housefly, the dragonfly, and the bee we encounter in daylight do not move in the same world that we observe them from, nor share with us nor with each other the same time and space.

Giorgio Agamben says that Uexküll says:
We assign vague names to things we use or need, as if they were mere objects without relativity. No animal can be associated with an object like that.

> *Goatself:*
> I eat half a tub of yogurt
> and call Ivan over
> to eat the rest.
> it's small for such a big snout.
> he licks it carefully
> and a little tediously
> his tongue sideways
> along the rim struggling
> contorting to touch the bottom
> down the steep sides adapting
> his tongue to the vessel
> with no knowledge of geometry.

the shepherd calls:
pen (*stani*)
sheep-pen (*stanotopi*)
goat-pen sheep-*stani* cattle-pen horse-pen
dog-pen
staniazo: to put inside the pen
to take out of the pen *xestaniazo*
field-pen
Oldpen Penplace Narrowpen
devil-pen
beggar-pen
stud-pen

graiki: animal camp
stalos: stall, stalling-place—of ample noon shade
mantri: pound
mantra: paddock
mantroula: little paddock
gidomandri: goat-paddock.

the proverb says:
keep your males
from your females.

the narrator says:
fold for goats for milking.
fold for kids for slaughtering.
fold for babies kept alive in order to give birth.
fold for males to be let out
two weeks in the spring
so the females become pregnant in unison
and while pregnant climb the mountain.
and while pregnant climb back down.
timed so that in October
they give birth and on Christmas
the kids are slaughtered and in February
the second group is born and at Easter
they are slaughtered and in May
the males are shorn and on the first week of June
during cheese-making season
they go up the mountain in a truck.
the division of everything as it corresponds to human needs.
the division of time as it corresponds.
the division of space time work utility
as it corresponds to their needs.
factory or labor camp.

Loukopoulos says:
Stack-stack-stack, like that
they topple the tops of firs, cedars, anything,
and pile them up to make a fence,
and when winter comes?
The same again: entire branches of trees, oaks
and paliurus shrubs—taken for the fold
which sting us now, you see—
to build a pen for the young.

Loukopoulos again:
So, a fence all around the area, two openings,
the entrance to the front pen here, the stone used as a milking seat there,
and that's the *strougga*.
A traveling pen.
You just drag the branches along, set it up farther away,
whatever works.

"I put the animals inside the strougga"
"a man is strougged (penned)"
"some wild goats got in the strougga"
"animals unstrougged the shepherd"
"you fuck shit mother-pen"
"holy pen!"
"shit pen!"
"see how they destrougged my beautiful field"
"the strougga is wrecked" he said
when his teeth fell out of his mouth.
after all, don't the teeth make a pen
to enclose the captive tongue?

narrator:
strougga: some boards and chicken wire.
inside go the males for shearing
starting with the biggest.
strong animals with twisting horns. the leaders

wearing heavy bells of different tones—a dozen—
on which they play
the chromatic scale.
patterns shorn on their fur.
ancient lines and surfaces.
unshorn patches harvested fields.
along the fence plastic coffee cups
one goat stretches
its neck over the fence to place its lips
on a frappe straw and sips.
Terry the Albanian shepherd tells me:
"she likes it very much and I let her
because she's my little one."

Uncle Yannis says:
I shear 800 goats by myself!
Whenever I want to, see this pair of scissors here
I'm, you know, a fanatic.
Don't believe me? Take me anywhere, any camp,
I'll show you how I shear them
I do it my way, you see,
like a working man!
Only a craftsman can cut designs like this!
You can try it too—
see, you're doing it like the children do when they give them a haircut.

and Uncle Yannis says:
I even cut women's hair. Maroula, she comes to me and says,
"Cut my hair."
"Get out of here, you're a woman. How am I supposed to cut your hair?"
"Eh, come on, cut it."
So I cut it.
"How pretty," she says.

Joseph Dacre Carlye and Philip Hunt say:
Small coins were tied into her braids, which fell down her back and

nearly touched the ground.

Uncle Yannis says:
the same way you dress a woman, the headscarf,
the coins, and so on,
it's like that when you dress the herds.
From the large bells to the small bells, all to show off
in a way that's most, most presentable.
When I'm inspired, I dress the animals how I want.
Like you say, I want to give myself
a good appearance, that's what I do for the herd,
give it an appearance.

Ami Boué says:
The Greeks and Tsindari Vlachs will sometimes sing in chorus, with one person making a nasal droning sound reminiscent of the bagpipe. Their obsession with singing can sometimes be unusual. Generally the flute is the accompanying instrument. Everywhere in Greece, shepherds can be heard in the fields, making wild melodies with their flutes to the gurgling of the waters and the rustling of wind through the trees.

narrator:
wooden utensils, the traveler writes
carved art, the folklorist says
that which is carved.
crossing ravines and mountains collecting bits of wood.
wood for drinking cups for ladles wood for collars
spindle whorls.
wood for the wooden stake in the ground the rod the spoons.
wood for the shepherd's crook. for flutes.

Loukopoulos says:
the shepherd never lets
the crook slip from his hand
he would endure
what a boatman endures

who loses his oar
on the open sea
were you to take
the crook from his hands
he'd be rudderless
lost
which is why he sleeps
clutching it
day and night.

Archilochus says:
by my spear the bread
by my spear
the Ismaric wine
which I drink
leaning against it
by this spear
scaffolded.

> *Goatself:*
> what difference a crook and a spear?

Loukopoulos says:
curved crook of the shepherd carved from oak, wild olive
I took it up
I left it
I built my nest against it
hung from it
hung myself from it
it is all of my belongings.

Giorgis Exarchos writes:
However, Leake noticed some of the flutes from Epirus were unique and hadn't yet been recorded. They were made from the feet of eagles or griffon vultures, because their bones were very hard and long enough to be used for a shepherd's flute.

They are somewhat more common today than in the ancient world, because it is easier to kill a griffon vulture with gunpowder than, say, a bow.

Flutes

in a time of idleness,
when the tender breeze
Zephyr
blows and caresses
their cheeks,
they sit in the thick shade
of a rock.
drinking milk
or wine.
lulled by the rustle
of leaves
and the tiny song of the cicada.
carving wood
or whistling.
but the best flute
isn't made of wood
but from the bones
of an eagle.
to make this music
you first needed to learn
how to fly.

Hymn to Swallow and Nightingale

of the nightingale in the leaves
                                              hidden
its cry
                                              motionless
grieving in the morning and at night
each tree a nightingale   voice
in dialogue with others
in other trees

motionless cocking its head
to answer with its purring throat—
                                              voicèd polyphony
with eyes fixated on the sky we seek

the extravagant the most unspoiled   and luminous
boughs the tender leaves
from our seats beneath the tree in the sunlight

though our view of the sky is clearer
the closer we are to the ground
                                              lying on my back
I marvel at the celestial singer
while underneath in the yard
the stones carrying the day's trapped heat
warm me
                                              it's getting late

the nightingale empties   the gladness
of the mouth   sounding
crying for its lost young
or a mate
boasting skyward with its outsized   voice
all but invisible

on the tallest branch
                              hovering
only *aman-aman*
mountain keening
voicings from the tender branches
shoot up
nourished by the waters of an invisible river

while the swallows sing only   in motion
when they fly they
scream midair
lacerate the blue   horizon
slash with their swordtails
the celestial   myriad

emitting shrill intermittent arrhythmic
joyful cries
grazing each other every now and then
as if to say
"my little swallow
there, in the distances where you reside."
we remain fastened to the land
while they
living creatures of the sky, flowers
in the air, toil away down our street
to build a single nest
each accompanying the other
with us   accompanied
they leave and return
leave and return
chitterings lullabies glidings
self-contained words   uttered
you of the unuttered   notes

swallow-reveling.

Sun and Night Stars

there is an observer narrator
there is my naked chest beneath the sun
the observer in present tense speaks in third person
for other beings
the sun singes, arouses
the observer speaks of the moon the glow of stars
the wind rain rain petals
crickets owls a cicada a fly
grass cherries mosquito
at times the narrator turns
and enters his words to confuse us
but I saw it: the white
shell of a cricket floating on the water surface
of the bucket in the garden
exoskeleton
illuminated by the sea and the stars of that particular
night
narrator it was yours, your old coat
your *geras* your cape your shield
tossed off, and from the fig tree
you perch in the well's eye
to gaze at
your reflection

5. WORKS AND DAYS

Uncle Yannis: The Vlach Road was straight. We'd pass through Pelekoudi, Gerakari, Tsoukka, Deskati, then from there on to Dimitra—not Dimitra damnit, Karpero, and Christo, Kalpidi, and Grevena; the way was straight.

MM: Thirty-five days in the fall.

UY: In the spring it was seventeen.

MM: In the fall the animals weren't pregnant, and were trying to be more ... economical.

UY: Seventeen days in the spring, versus thirty-five. Sometimes forty. One time in the road we did in forty days, an old man came out and said "forty days, eighty-five loaves."

MM: Loaves! From cracked wheat.

UY: Well, what bread we had we made into hardtack.

MM: We'd tear up the loaves and bake them again, into hardtack that would last for days. Forty days!

UY: But now we go up the mountain in trucks, as you see.

Aristotle says:
Which is why there are so many different types of animals and humans, and as it's impossible to live without food, the lives of animals differ depending on their food, and it's the same with humans. The nomadic are the most idle, because feeding their stock is nearly effortless, and when it is time to change pastures for them, they too must also follow, because they are cultivators of a living crop.

Léon Heuzey says:
The Vlach one meets in Acarnania is, on the contrary, the archetype of a nomad. Movement for him isn't an obligation he suffers, but a necessity, it is his life itself. I don't know what kind of spirit of change and motion courses the veins of the Vlach-Aromanians. Untethered from the soil where others stay as if rooted, where he's acquired, we might say, his nature from his herds that, every year, drive him up the mountains and back down into valleys. There's a common superstition among them, according to which if one of them were to settle down somewhere, and buy land and build a house, he'd soon grow sick and waste away, and become food for worms.

Henri Belle says:
Even on their mountains, in summer, while the women and children remain in their huts, the men wander the high plateaus with their dogs, changing their pastures each day and sleeping outdoors wrapped in woolen cloaks, indifferent to the sun, the rain, exhaustion, and hardship, living in a wild state in the company of hawks and rocks, ignoring every progress and advance of civilization, scorning any other work, ignoring all but the money they receive from selling their goats and cheeses.

Pouqueville says:
They apportion time according to the phases of rural life, such as the kidding season, shearing time, and official religious holidays. On the feast day of Agios Georgios, which marks the start of the pastoral year, they celebrate with their families and roast the lambs that were born too early. The return of the swallows and the May nymph that blind

minstrels sing to, traveling village to village, heralds the season of flowers and the florid days of April.

Chara says:
I walked through your door
you tried to play it off
but I could tell right away
you'd been eating garlic.

The song goes:
It is best to be a donkey in May
a ram in June
a cat in January
and a rooster always.

Uncle Yannis says:
A human life: if someone kept a diary from the day they're born till the last day, it would say, I lived. How could you argue with that? You couldn't say oh they lived like this, or had this specific life. No. It's bigger than that.

Henri Bell says:
In autumn, when the north wind brings the first snows as a harbinger of heavy winter to come, they descend back down into the valleys. In spring, when the scorching heat that is fatal to the animals begins, and the young goats have been sold for Easter, they slowly ascend back into the cold airs from which winter had driven them.

Stamatia, on the train to Athens, says:
a very mixed autumn this year for us
sometimes clouds sometimes light rain
maybe that's why it's snowing now
this year we had a very mixed autumn
at Christmas there were days
that felt like Easter

you don't know what the wind was like that wind
brought down all the trees
tore our tarps
so I'm rushing around
and manage to save up eight containers this year

in winter if you don't have a reason don't travel

what nature provides is good
change is good
everyone needs change
what's your name?
my name is Stamatia
usually I travel at night
so I can be home by morning
I have a little girl
she carries a bag soooo big
the bottom of her feet are swollen
like bread

I really like to get home the night before
to air out the house, to cook

you're by yourself every day, no?
why not be on holiday too?

they say:
when the moon sleeps
the shepherd stays awake.

When the moon is up
the shepherd sleeps.

Passov recorded the song "Sea Bird and Mountain Bird":
a bird from the sea and a bird from the mountain
were fighting, were fighting

for the mountain, the pasture, the shore;
the sea bird says to the mountain bird:
"Go back to your place, bird, go back to your people.
I've put up with you too long, I won't do it anymore."
"Don't yell at me, bird, stop trying to shoo me away,
I'm only staying here a little while.
Perhaps May through June and July
and maybe five days in August or maybe six or ten,
then I'm off, back home to my own."

Pouqueville says:
The bleating of the goats, the yelps of the dogs, and the shouts and banging of the shepherds gave a special music to this moving phalanx of people and animals from Pindos to the valleys of Macedonia and Thessaly.

Like the storks, those famous migrating birds that travel far from their home and their nests, taking their new families with them over lands and seas, the Vlachs push onwards with the hope that next year they'll once again find their homes and those they left behind.

the narrator (spring equinox on a bus on the highway):
again the yellow fields
the heavy heat the farm machinery the olives
shining in wind
Misko numero 1 in Greece
light in columns and shafts from gray
clouds bearing rain
the summer water
thunder smells of earth
LINET industries
Assos boilers
Stasinopoulos Timber Formica
BLK Aluminum
Rouchotas Timber Parquet
Rough-Hewn Marble
oil drums

and now rain
a shepherd holding his crook
off the highway
white oleander blossoms
cimarelli cimarelli olive shakers
dense cornfields
butcher-slash-taverna
Krokio Public School
gas station
fields road and sea
wood pellets coal
wall of corn
corn barley for sale
prepackaged or in bulk
river bends and now bridge
figs reeds and plane trees
rest stop
garden bed with veggies
harvested field boustrophedon
mama said to get sweet acacia for the house
Locker Room
and vineyards
Pelion Stone Hearths
The Reunion Bar & Grill
blue tiles on the wall
Organic Vineyards or K T E O
A I P E gas station
nameless gas station
unknown gas station
Volos 20 kilometers
animal feed oleander
sweet acacia and mulberry she told me
but the roots don't fit anywhere

Yannis Tsevrechos says:
The goats are incompatible with the enclosure's stale air, so they stare

out through the slats. Even in winter, no matter how bad the weather gets, the goat wants to see it for itself, even if it can only stand half an hour outside. Even if it has everything it needs, food and water, inside.

Pouqueville says:
We saw long lines of sheep and goats, followed by a solitary shepherd playing the flute and walking behind.

the breeder says:
They have developed a sense of navigation I tell you, if you leave them somewhere, they can get back again, they know how to move in a way that finds the path of least resistance, the clear path, they read a place, its geography, they're in sync with nature, born in nature. This we saw but never experienced ourselves, which is why we changed professions.

Joseph Dacre Carlyle and Philip Hunt say:
Walking in the street with their swaddled babies on their backs, balancing a large jar or urn on their heads while all the time twining the distaff, winding the spindle.

Demetris Letsios the photographer says:
We traveled on foot and at night on the way to Agrafa because during the day there were airplanes. We walked through the fields at night. But this life was also good. The role played by women in the fields during the resistance was important.

Apostolos Bardas says:
we Vlachs are like birds
come March and April and we're gone
mountainward.

Vlach proverb:
Τάστουρλου ντι-ν-ανούμιρα σι φούγγα.
(Bag on the shoulder and go.)

Morning Epilogue

this summer.
I lived with loved ones.
I walked in the forest.
this summer.
we didn't swim in the sea
but entered it and sat for hours
talking while rotating our feet
just enough to float.
we climbed on the horses
went berry picking
let time pass as it wanted
without forcing.
Ivan
our new dog brought us here.
after I'd finished
L'esprit du Zen
the first and last book
of the summer
Ivan stole it like he does
tore it apart with his teeth.
pages leaves bits of fragments
text
drifted across the yard
carried off by wind.
I kept trying to grab them
as they were leaving.
how to walk in the spirit of zen?
how to move through the world
coherently
when all your verbs
are past tense
and the stars that you see
went out an eternity ago.

the loss—possession
the past—belonging to now
as memory to oblivion.
the almond between your teeth is earth.

Morning Hot and Windless

spread out along the olive tree like a drawn bow.
my back against the tree
my abdomen against the sky
hands uplifted
feet open to winds
suspended in the world
while everywhere the endless drone
of cicadas in chorus
alone I prowled away from the others
for hours splitting the air
with my strange and sad desire's
keen.
o sea of olives and noonday stone
above the bright sea of goats out
to the shining Aegean
farther out
to the horizon's secret end.

6. CHIMERA

Yannis Mourtos: You saw why I was there for the birth. I was pulling out the goat. Step by step.
   All of this is love, my little one. Like nothing else in life.

the narrator says:
I was still little when I saw a cow giving birth
on the steep slopes of the mountain
saw the eyes
as soon as it left the womb
shining with fluids
trembling it stood on its thin legs
for human children it takes a year to walk.

Yannis Mourtos says:
After it happened to me, I mean since I learned about birth, how animals give birth, there in the tractor the woman gave birth, I cut the cord a little longer and tied it with the string from a pompom hanging from the mirror.

Makis Mourtos says:
Don't be shocked by what he says about a woman giving birth on the route. In those days most women gave birth that way. On the route. They set out from here for seventeen to twenty days at a time, and if a woman was pregnant and far along, she'd give birth on the route. There was no hospital to go to, or anything else.

narrator:
Sometimes there are new mothers who don't want the baby. They won't feed them. To discipline the mothers they remove them from the flock. They confine them for one or two days in a 5' x 5' enclosure with their kids. Till they get used to it, and are forced to give their milk.

Transhumance I

for Eleonora and Dimitris

It was I who sent
my treasure
by my own free will
silently I step upon the earth

i.
In the beginning was the grazing
the pasture, sections of earth gathered extended
suffused from rain and the elements
eaten
by footsteps, the cursive of animals and humans
echoing
the valleys, streams, and summits beyond
brought back voices.

ii.
In the beginning was the field.
To move out I had to gather.
I had to cull
the things.
The things, the animals, the things, the things.

iii.
— What do you carry on you when you leave?
— My dark. My own piece of dark.
— What do you carry when you leave?
— The markings on the body.
— What do you carry when you leave?
— My spell:
Forgot–tenacts–forgot–tenwords
fragme–ntsof–theform–erlife
tokeep–ascharm–tokeep–asnew–redcru–cifix.

iv.
—To move on I had to cull
the things, the fragments
my children
left behind
before leaving me to begin their own lives.

v.
— *Kiatra kraapa omlou nou kriapa*
(A stone breaks, a man does not break.)

vi.
— Still
the fragments are glass
pressed deep under skin
traveling in the flesh
choosing their own paths,
one ascends to the heart,
another pierces your abdomen.

— What does God cast down that the earth does not swallow?
— Wound through and through.
I spit it from my mouth like a bitter seed
but not a single teardrop touched my cheek,
why I had for years now
clenched my teeth.

— You cannot eat a stone, mother says
instead of
you cannot escape your fate.
— In order to leave
I had to cull the things.
That agony lasted months.
An entire winter.
Heavy and dark, stripping layer by layer
the vessels of memory.

But what hurt most
was what had, for so long, slipped
between my fingers like air.
What had been forgotten.
The missing.
What had not happened.

— Λεῦσσε δ' ὅμως ἀπεόντα νόῳ παρεόντα βεβαίως

Parmenides says:
but see with your mind those who are missing, as if
they were present.

vii.
—And the upbringing was over. the departure performed.
absence a native plant sprouting
separation a self-growing pain
seed without water roots in secret
distance-nurtured
what you didn't do hurts more
than what was done
spring arrives. for a moment the darkness
is paused.
and I can leave. lighter.
I carried as little as possible
most I left behind in rooted houses.
of motherhood.
my home is transient.
I carry with me only a few boxes
fragments of the former life
pictures and writings
for use in
my solitary
ceremony
of unbinding tears.

viii.
To leave I had to gather the things
beneath my feet the earth was leaving
it takes time to uproot from one's place.
it takes time to leave a life's worth of wrappers.
it takes time to disentangle from your children's roots.
but you don't.
I made the wrong association.
children's things equal the children themselves
who've left.
uprooted already. what I keep is mine.
you said: don't throw them away, they're memories.
(and I believed you'd remain small always believed
the moment would stay)
and you kept: broken toys bits of paper
cards and tickets pictures magazines
fragments
books a ceramic pot you once painted
a tin box filled with paper
a piggy bank shaped like a red bus
plastic dragons soldiers torn posters
more dragons. paintings of dragons.
pieces stuck to the wall.
and you kept: photographs of actors
pen sketches on notebook paper
pictures of your summer vacation
your favorite band which changed and changed again
a model with a huge bag that read:
"I never find what I'm looking for"
a scrap of paper that said *only love matters*
that you taped to the wardrobe.
the bedroom walls were friezes
triglyphs and metopes
ornamented
with your own mythos
apotropaic charms against fear

ornament of intimacy.
I took them down one by one.
some so old they tore.
some I put in the box.
the walls stripped naked.
and painted for the next tenants.
new traces applied to them.
nothing will say what the house was for us
or what unknown beautiful children grew up
in it.
to move on I had to throw your things away.

ix.
To move on I had to gather my things.
to remember to consider I had to think
to abandon.
what I could gather I gathered
what I could keep I kept
time can't repeat no going back to live it again
at this task I was properly lost.
wounded.
mother is a wound.

x. *Wish*
I cry just two times a year now
it starts when I'm asleep
you're small and tender and cool to the touch
like water
and when I wake I'm already crying
because you've grown
how far you are now.
may your heart always remain tender
in your large body.
and your life be long
and lucky and joyful.
"with my blessing," grandma would say
when we told her goodbye. go.

Noon

for El

I heard your voice
upstairs. there's a scorpion
in the bathroom.
and picked out
a fat tome
The Neverending Story
from the bookshelf
of the orphanage: what you and your friends called
that cramped chamber
with its two single beds and little icon
on the headboard,
and hurled it at him.
we stomped on the cover
again and again
until the life was gone.
always
my daughter
you are the one to find them.
you'd seen it years ago
in the darkness near the spring
beside the plane trees and cistern
the giant scorpion.
the bitterness of its venom drawn to sweetness.
wishing to join in a single word.
bittersweet.
mother's daughter
rushing water.
when the Kore uproots
gone from the earth
of Demeter. of the mother.

7. SACRIFICE

Uncle Yannis: You see. Man is a beast. If he wants something, he takes it. Because now, with the crisis, the one who wants to get ahead will get ahead. The one who doesn't, never will.

>*Goatself:*
>river full of stars will you hear me?
>I came down the ridge to speak to you,
>along the shores of your tributaries spiders dance
>weaving unraveling life
>dance of unraveling wherein Athena
>faces Dionysus.

the narrator:
a goat gave birth to a dead kid
in its place they gave her a sheep
a sheep growing up among goats
won't have a good fate,
says the goatherd.

>*Goatself:*
>I remember watching you
>as you were going down the ridge
>when the bells were ringing all at once
>like a voice
>of one accord.

the narrator elaborates:
he bisects the throat with a knife
cuts with a handsaw the horns
inserts a tube
through a hole between the skin and the flesh
inflates it with a pump
to begin separating with his fingers skin from flesh
he cuts away the front extremities
folds the skin inside out
removes the hide from the back feet (now upwards)
towards the head (downwards now)
the knife reaches the head, pares away the skin
from the cheeks the mouth the ears

with one last flick he dissevers it and tosses it aside
suspending the pelt on the hook by the tendons of the feet

his is an absolute precision he is the dancer

bisects with the knife from throat to clavicle
bisects vertically the stomach in the middle
tugs out the large intestine tosses it aside
tugs out the viscera the hearts stomachs all together.
— how little were you when you learned to do this?
— very little. Look, it's best to learn it all when you're very little.
Rips the abdomen and tugs out the heart the viscera
coils the intestine in a spool,
sets aside a piece of stomach for the rennet,
cuts the head,
halves the body end to end
whatever lands on the ground
is food for the chickens and dogs
from each half he cuts away the feet
cutting the ribs one by one
in motions of absolute precision he is the dancer.

Homer says:
and near us the goatherd Melanthius passed by
leading the finest goats
from each herd to give a feast
for the suitors,
and two shepherds followed him.

Walter Burkert on sacrifice in ancient Greece:
the blood must never touch the ground
if the animal is small, they hoist it above the altar,
or else collect its blood in a designated vessel
and with it anoint the altar stone
which must at all times ceaselessly leak blood.
The animal is cut in sections and its viscera removed.

The uses for each portion
are strictly determined by tradition.
First they place the still-beating heart on the altar.
A seer is always on hand
to read the lobes of the liver.
Quickly they scorch the guts in the altar's flame
and devour them piping hot.
Only the gallbladder is left uneaten.
Meanwhile the femurs
along with the pelvis and the tailbone
are laid on the altar "in orderly fashion."
The arrangement of the bones indicates
their interrelation
the members of the living animal
and its primary form is restored
as sacred.

Homer says:
And now they laughed as though from lips not their own
bloodstained from the meat they had eaten, their eyes
filled with tears, and in their minds it was as if they were grieving.

Regarding those who are buried without a funeral, Exarchos offers:
After the day of execution people heard frequently,
around the time of midnight, voices, the cries
and screams of the fighters:
—*Ouleleleleee, oulelele, oulelelelelelelee...*

Overheard among the shepherds:
—the number of males you keep depends on the size of your herd, for
each male there must be a certain number of females.
—how many females for 15 males?
—about five times that.
—ah, five times.
—one male suffices for twenty females.
—one male twenty females.

Goatself:
its eyes still bleary the newborn goat
is searching for my finger to suck
my finger
and heart
are glad.

and later we will drink
its mother's milk
meant for it.

the shepherd says:
when the children leave the mothers grieve.

Transhumance II

for mama

i.
words are markings on the mountains
the mountains aren't spoken
the words are plaited tracks
the words are branches
the place flashes through time
time does not exist
time turns back
each year I ascend and descend your line
time
carrying nothing on my back
I stitch I unravel joy through sorrow
carrying each day on my back.

ii.
in the beginning was the law: scraps of earth allotted
how far? up to the markings
each time a little farther out
beyond.

iii.
boats of people leave in droves
young and strong
their mothers in their headscarves left behind
wondering "where are you now, my son?"
daily and praying
in the light,
will they find out in the end?
"where are you, my son," the goddess Thetis asks,
a cuttlefish or cormorant
diving into the sea
like a bird in the sky

"I nursed you with rosewater
raised you with milk
with my immortal fire
I submerged you within it
to be a shield for your body for when you're beyond my reach
but bodies are bodies, they're tangible
and I had to hold you by the ankles
upside down
from your tiny heels
and this stamp this undying grip
became your vulnerable marking, my dear
the place of the mother's grip
the mark of death."

iv.
they called and said
come over
when I got there a young shepherd
stood inside the pen a tall redhead
in a cobalt blue uniform choosing
kids for slaughter
males mostly, two months old
he took them one by one in his arms
and while they bleated walked over
cross dangling over his chest
and carried them across the fence
to the other side
he was Christ and Calf Bearer
and Charon
but also he was midwife
and mother he knew
by heart whose child was which
having guided with his hands
each one's mouth to its mother's breast
he showed it how
and even taught the mother

what to do
now he shoves each one inside
the black opening of the truck bed
the mouth that would
take them to Hades
and when
one manages to nudge
its tiny head through the hole he stops
to caress
it lovingly before hitting
its nose back in
when the mothers return to the pen
from pasture
and find them gone
inconsolable—he tells me—they grieve
do they realize?
will they remember?

EPILOGUE

narrator:
On the 23rd of May 2016, the herd of Yannis Mourtos was sold.

Darkness Again

for years the dead didn't bother us
we tucked them one by one into the earth
from which
often the most recent
would visit us
usually in our sleep and without warning
empty-handed
like memory's beggars
their gaze and voice
and sudden appearance
at our door
were sometimes frightening
other times comforting
gradually emptiness tugged them
beyond reach
always further and further out
merging with the nonexistent
remnants
of an enveloping cosmos
of which we know nothing
or can even conceive
far shadows of a dream
that we forgot
but never once
did their blood stop reaching
still deeper
through the same quirks, the same demeanor
and forgotten antics
that belonged to us,
or were they theirs alone?
for years the dead didn't bother us
then the pains began
and love

which woke them and made them
reach out their hands again
to us and night
to their song from nowhere
their own nowhere inside
our here and now
blood, earth, flesh, bone,
and joint heart abiding.

the cantor says:
each action each thought each state of each being
that passed through the world
does it exist now and always?
do they raise into the sky like hands like branches
voices coalescing repeating from their first hour
of utterance?
does each one's walking or swimming
or moving through the air sound in unison
from the first, unchanging?
are new voices yet added
to their song?
we return to find
the ones who come
over and over with weapons without weapons
with another step another hoof fall
the beauty of the virgins
in the battle of Alcman.

from the General State Archives:
ANSWER: One night, three days before being discharged, slaves entered the village Sourpi, and the three of us, thieves, were staying around the village and went into the houses and took bread. [...] In the evening we went down again and were given food by the coal-burner Vlachs and stayed among the sheepfold in a place I don't know the name of.

QUESTION: Why have you taken up a life of thievery?

ANSWER: To become rich.

QUESTION: You know how to read and write?

ANSWER: I know, yes, but I cannot sign because my hand is wounded and in pain.

Notes

VOICES

Edmond About (French traveler, novelist and journalist, 1828–1885)
Giorgio Agamben (Italian philosopher)
Argos (the mythic dog of Odysseus)
Eleonora Antonakaki-Giannisi (Greek PhD candidate in German Philosophy, the narrator's daughter)
Dimitris Antonakakis-Giannisis (Greek musician, the narrator's son)
Archilochus (ancient Greek lyric poet from Paros, perhaps a mythic figure, first a cow breeder then a mercenary soldier, 680–645 BCE)
Aristotle (ancient Greek philosopher, 384–322 BCE)
Melpo Axioti (Greek poet and writer, 1905-1973)
Apostolos Bardas (Vlach shepherd)
Henri Belle (French diplomat in Athens, 1837–1908)
Ami Boué (French Huguenot traveler, geologist, 1794–1881)
Walter Burkert (German scholar of Greek mythology, religions, and cults, 1931–2015)
Joseph Dacre Carlyle and Philip Hunt (English travelers, the first an Orientalist, 1758–1804, and the second, a priest who helped Lord Elgin take the Parthenon Marbles, 1772–1838)
Matsi Chatzilazarou (beloved female Greek poet, 1914–1987)
Edward Daniel Clarke (English traveler, clergyman, naturalist, mineralogist, 1769–1822)
Cyclops (ancient Greek mythic creatures with one eye, goat herders)
Jacques Derrida (French philosopher, 1930–2004)
Leonidas Embeirikos (Greek historian and linguist)
Giorgis Exarchos (Vlach anthologist and writer)
Empedocles (Greek pre-Socratic philosopher from Akragas c. 492–432 BCE)
General State Archives
Goatself
Giorgos Giannisis (Greek biologist)
Grandmother (narrator's maternal grandmother, Maria Kandri, from a breeding village in the Peloponnese)
Donna Haraway (US philosopher, biologist, eco-feminist)
Léon Heuzey (French traveler, archaeologist, historian, 1831–1922)
Homer (ancient Greek epic oral poets going as back as far as a millennium BCE, transcribed in a written version centuries later, perhaps in the 6th

century BCE)

Ivan (the narrator's dog)

Panagiotis Karakanas (Vlach cheese maker in Volos)

Maria Kokkinou and Andreas Kourkoulas (Greek architects)

Thanasis Koutinas (singer and teacher of Vlach polyphony)

William Martin Leake (British traveler, military officer and classical scholar, topographer of ancient cities, 1777–1860)

Dimitris Letsios (member of the Greek resistance to the Nazis and photographer from Volos, 1910–2008)

Henry George Liddell (1811–1898) and Robert Scott (1811–1887) (British classical scholars, authors of *A Greek-English Lexicon*, first published in 1843)

Dimitris Loukopoulos (Greek folklorist from Roumeli, 1874–1943)

Iris Lykourioti (Greek architect and designer)

Yannis Mavrakakis (Cretan folklorist, 1940–2021)

Mother (Kaiti Giannisi)

Andreas Moukas (Greek breeder, Mount Parnassus, voice recording from the Melpo and Octave Merlier Archive)

Makis Mourtos (MM, Yannis Mourtos' nephew, ex-breeder from Aetomilitsa-Denitsko)

Narrator

Yannis Mourtos (UY or Uncle Yannis, breeder, goat-herd owner from Aetomilitsa, seventy years old)

Parmenides (Greek pre-Socratic philosopher and poet, *c*. 515–*c*. 450 BCE)

Arnold Passov (German Hellenist who collected Greek folk songs, 1829–1870)

Plato (ancient Greek philosopher from Athens, *c*. 428–*c*. 348 BCE)

François Charles Hugues Laurent Pouqueville (French traveler, diplomat, explorer, physician, 1770–1838)

Stamatia (a train passenger)

Chara Stergiou (Greek architect, artist)

Thetis (mythic mother of the hero Achilles and a goddess of the sea)

Yannis Tsevrechos (from the village of Diasello in Thessaly, a goatherd, author of *The Flock*)

Giorgos Tzirtzilakis (Greek art curator, critic, and historian)

Jakob Johann Freiherr von Uexküll (Baltic German biologist, 1864–1944)

Alan John Bayard Wace (1879–1957) and Maurice Scott Thompson (1884–1971) (British archaelogists, authors of *The Nomads of the Balkans*, 1914)

X and X2 (goatherds)

You

ETYMOLOGY

Goatself is a name given by a former teacher combining "ego (I)" and its homophone *aigo* (goat)." If the etymology of "ego" is "edo" (here), a place implying "me," then Goatself signifies a multiplicity of beings that live in this place and share the speaker's voice.

Nomad: member of a people traveling from place to place to find pasture for its animals. More generally, a wanderer. In plural: pastoral tribes, also of the Cyclopes. From the Greek νομ-άς , άδος, ὁ, ἡ, the one that is roaming about for pasture. Comes from the verb νέμω (nemo),
    I. distribute, share, allot, distribute in groups
    II. generally, enjoy
    III. recite
    IV. of herdsmen, pasture, to graze their flocks, drive to pasture

As also νόμος, ὁ (nomos)
    I. usage, custom
    II. melody, strain
    III. in modern Greek: law

Song (tragoudi), n.
    I. a canticle, small goat. From *tragodia*, tragedy, goat song: a Chorus consisting of Goats.

Tragedy (tragodia), f.
    I. the dramatic genre that flourished in ancient Athens during the fifth century, structured in various parts. It combined verses, song, music, and orchestration, and was performed as an official religious and political event in the theatre of Dionysus by male actors and a male chorus, citizens of Athens. According to Aristotle, its purpose was to make the audience feel strong emotions of pity and fear, culminating in catharsis.
    II. a work that belongs to that genre.
    III. a modern theatrical work that has a sad story.
    IV. (concurrently) a tragic event.

Instead of tragedy, Aigedy.
From *aix, aigos* (αἴξ , αἰγός, ὁ, ἡ) :
    i. *goat*, mostly fem.,
    II. αἴξ Ἄγριος wild *goat*

III. plural, *waves*

The Aegean Sea (*ΑΙΓΑΙΟ ΠΕΛΑΓΟΣ*) is derived from *aix*, and so is *Kataigis* (the storm).

PROVERBS

"goats are plow-free": for those who have been relieved of some weight (because the free nature of goats makes it impossible for them to be attached to plows)
"to the wild goats" : to the crow (to hell)
"goat names": of worthless objects.

Names of goats according to their color:
Arapou
Aspronourou
Flora
Florakanouto
Floro
Gaitanou
Galani
Geso
Giosa
Gormpo
Griva
Kanouta
Kanouto
Kavrelou
Kokkia
Kokkinomata
Koula
Laggonou
Laia
Liara
Liaro
Liopra
Matoulou
Mavri
Mavrokefalo
Mavrosfaiki
Melani

Mourakia
Mourna
Mouschro
Mouskouri
Mpalia
Mpaliatsoukou
Mpartsa
Mpartzo
Mpellia
Mpellou
Mpoutska
Paliri
Pestra
Podarousio
Prentzia
Psaria
Reikou
Rousa
Rouso
Spakou
Tsoukou
Vakrakia
Zarkad
Zonou

Names of goats according to their horns:
Klourokerato
Koutsokera
Krouta
Monokerati
Mproustoukera
Pisokera
Siouta
Stifanoukera
Striftokera
Traousio
Tsapaloukera
Tsiougka

Names of goats according to their udders:
Apalarmechti
Fouradomastari
Kalamoviza
Kalamovrizou
Kountoumastari
Koutlomastari
Makriviza
Mounouviza
Sfichtarmechti
Tsimporoviza
Tsimprovizou
Xountrouviza

According to their ears:
Lagofites
Mpalouchtres
Tsoupres

And more names for goats:
Apokonto
Arfani
Diplares
Falakri
Grammatou
Koutsounourla
Krouta
Ksanthoprosopi
Lagou
Lefka
Liafta
Liventou
Makraftou
Miksiasmeno
Mita
Morfou
Moukla
Mourka
Mouroucheiliasmeni
Mpafoukiasmeno

Mparezou
Mpovoulou
Niatou
Ntrenia
Palioflora
Paliogormpa
Paliokanouta
Pianoumeni
Tsimpidou
Virgi

Yannis Tsevrechos says:
Women used to lose their names
since the world called them
by the name of their husband.

Acknowledgments

HOMERICA

Thanks to the editors of the following magazines and journals where versions of these translations first appeared: *Arion, Beloit Poetry Journal, Columbia Journal, Crevice, The Stockholm Review,* and *World Literature Today.*

CICADA

Grateful acknowledgment is made to the magazines and journals in which some of these translations first appeared: *Parentheses*, PEN America, *Two Lines*, and *World Literature Today*

CHIMERA

For Kaiti, my mother.

Grateful acknowledgment is made to the following publications in which some of these translations first appeared:

Asymptote, "Prelude: Gray March Sky," "Transhumance I"
Denver Quarterly, "Noon," "Hymn to Swallow and Nightingale"
Guernica, "Noon"
Modern Poetry in Translation, "Noon"
Poetry, "Morning Hot and Windless," "Rumination"
The Southern Review, "Morning Epilogue"
World Literature Today, "Cyclops"

Chimera was funded in part by a National Endowment for the Arts Literature Translation Fellowship.

Thanks to all the Vlach goat herders of Kalamaki Larisis who opened their pens and accepted the Goatself and Narrator's presence, even in delicate moments, such as the mass birth delivery: mainly Yannis, Makis, Miltos, and Nikos Mourtos, and also Tasos Lagas and Lefteris Digos. Because *Chimera* is literally a polyphonic and multilingual work, which had to be shortened in size, the translation and editing of the project were particularly difficult and time-consuming. Goatself would like to express her gratitude to both the translator Brian Sneeden for undertaking the arduous effort and all his wonderful work once more, and to editor Declan Spring for his patience, his careful reading of many different versions, and his decisive contribution at all stages of the publication, and to Rachael Allen, whose brilliant vision and editorial guidance for this work has been indispensable. And finally: to Goatself's children, Eleonora and Dimitris, and friends Stathis Gourgouris, and Michaeljohn Raftopoulos, for their immense help and contributing remarks regarding the English-language versions of the work. And since this is (among other things) a book about companionship, Goatself shall remember, nor could she forget, her partner Zissis Kotionis, for sharing together bread and wine. This project appeared previously in various forms: in several poetic performances, an exhibition with Iris Lycourioti (*AIGAL O: The Songs*, Aggeliki Chatzimichali Museum, Athens, 2015), and a performance lecture in the Antigone Onassis Festival (*Nomos: The Land Song*, New York, 2016), directed by Isabella Martzopoulou.

Translations of epigraphs where a translator hasn't been attributed were translated by Brian Sneeden.

This book is printed with plant-based inks on materials certified by the Forest Stewardship Council®. The FSC® promotes an ecologically, socially and economically responsible management of the world's forests. This book has been printed without the use of plastic-based coatings.

The authorised representative in the EEA is eucomply OÜ, Pärnu mnt 139b-14, 11317 Tallinn, Estonia.
hello@eucompliancepartner.com
Tel. +33757690241